Help! My Husband is Hardly Home

HELP!

MY HUSBAND IS
HARDLY HOME

*8 Steps to Feel
Supported While Raising
Your Family*

KELSEY DOMIANA

NEW YORK

LONDON • NASHVILLE • MELBOURNE • VANCOUVER

Help! My Husband is Hardly Home

8 Steps to Feel Supported While Raising Your Family

© 2021 Kelsey Domiana

Published in New York, New York, by Morgan James Publishing in partnership with Difference Press. Morgan James is a trademark of Morgan James, LLC. www.MorganJamesPublishing.com

ISBN 9781642799019 paperback
ISBN 9781642799026 eBook
ISBN 9781642799033 audio
Library of Congress Control Number: 2019953682

Cover Design: Christopher Kirk www.GFSstudio.com

Interior Design: Chris Treccani www.3dogcreative.net

Editor: Todd Hunter

Author Photo by: Nathan Clark

Book Coaching: The Author Incubator

Morgan James is a proud partner of Habitat for Humanity Peninsula and Greater Williamsburg. Partners in building since 2006.

Get involved today! Visit
MorganJamesPublishing.com/giving-back

I dedicate this to myself.
This is your reclamation, Kelsey Domiana.

Also, this is for my Honey Buns. Had you been
home more often, this book wouldn't be possible.

Table of Contents

Acknowledgments

I would like to thank all of the women in my life. Each and every one of you has taught me something about myself, and I am so grateful to have learned from all of you.

Shout out to you, Mom. You are the most supportive person I know. Thank you for always answering my phone calls even when you are in important meetings and workout classes. You are such an incredibly loving, powerful, and beautiful woman. I appreciate you more than you could imagine, and I thank God for your being.

Memommy, Aunt Mel, Aunt Val, Darienne, Kelly, and Danyele—all of you have shaped me into the woman I am today whether you know it or not. Thanks for being examples of phenomenal women. I love you all so much.

And to my Juni Love, you are my greatest teacher. You are true to your name. Despite your journey, you never compromise your integrity. You gave me the courage to be my authentic self and share my story. You make me proud to be your mama, and I am honored you chose me to guide you Earth side. I am humbled to be able to share in your ancestral wisdom.

Thank you, Jada, for trusting in me to help you navigate through your journey toward healing. You were with me during the grassroots, which would not have been able to flourish without you.

Jemini, you are such a light in my life. Thank you for your continued support, teaching, and accountability throughout.

And Lara. I said your name, happy? That's enough of an acknowledgment for you. Kidding. Thank you for your open ears, open arms, and open heart. Also, thanks for giving me my nephews—Manboy, Jaxsonian, and Mr. Burrito. They are beyond blessed to have you as their mama.

Dad, you are one of my biggest cheerleaders and my biggest advocate. We've come a long way, and I value our relationship more than ever before.

Thanks, David for keeping it real and logical, as always. You told me, but I had to experience it in order to really know.

Chandler, thank you for loving me despite actually knowing the real me and for being in my corner always. My guy.

Thank you to Angela Lauria and The Author Incubator's team, as well as to David Hancock and the Morgan James Publishing team for helping me bring this book to print.

Last but not least, thank you to my loving and generous husband and soul mate, Maurice. I am forever grateful for your constant encouragement, unwavering faith in me, and unconditional love. You always see the strength in me. Thank you for being so supportive through all of this. I love you, Honey Buns. Bisou.

Chapter 1

Am I the Only One Feeling This Way?

You are playing the supportive role to your husband and his career while raising your family. Where do you fit in with all of that? How do you maintain your identity when your entire world revolves around your husband's career and your children's needs? The challenges you may face are endless. There are tons of situations you have encountered or are likely to encounter.

You wake up exhausted from a day that hasn't even begun. You are overwhelmed with the endless responsibilities that fall solely on you. Life has spiraled out of control, and you can never seem to catch up on housework and that never-ending to-do list. You are depleted and your children are sucking the life out of you, literally and/or figuratively. You are sad and can't quite figure out why. You are not the most pleasant person to be around. You look run-down and haggard. You feel down, unfulfilled, and empty but don't know how to lift yourself up. You have lost yourself at some point along the way, and you're unsure of how you reached this dark place.

Maybe you did not want to be in a lonely partnership or thought you would never be carrying what feels like all of the weight of the family responsibilities. You've probably said some variation of . . .

"I'm over it."

"I didn't sign up for this."

"I can't bear this anymore."

"I didn't think it would be like this."

Perhaps you can't really talk to anyone about what you are going through because they don't get it. They think you live a luxurious basketball-wife life, do nothing all day, and get the privilege to stay at home—which is only their perception, not your actual reality nor truth.

You are isolated in a city away from everyone you know and love, and your husband's gone on long, road game stretches. Or maybe you see him in clumps—a day, weeks, or months at a time because he works the second shift, two jobs, or is back in school. You are bothered by the attention your man gets from other women when the only attention you get is from your littles, asking everything of you and, well, your man—but he's not really around to answer. It makes you feel like what you are doing is not enough.

Your kids are on a schedule, so you feel comfortable scheduling something for yourself during naptime, but of course, that particular day, they don't go down for a nap at the regular time. Or, maybe you have to scramble to make your midterm paper deadline, but your son's sixth sense flares up, and her instantly becomes fussy and clingy instead of playing by himself as he normally does. Or when you are "touched out," and in order to feel human again, you just need two minutes to yourself without any tiny fingers jabbing into your thighs, bodies tackling you, or a little face pressing up against your face. Or your kids won't listen, and you are about to explode.

I am almost positive you yearn for some form of physical touch from your spouse—hugs, kisses, holding hands, cuddling, waking up next to him in the morning. You could be pregnant and just want a belly rub from his meaty, strong hands. You desire for his finger to interlace with yours or for him to curl up next to you on the couch. Maybe you need that emotional support and reassurance from him because you feel deflated.

You can't help but cry sometimes because you miss your husband so much. Maybe you have attended a wedding alone and seen all the other couples around you and wished he were there with you. You and your kids are out experiencing life and want to live all those moments with him, but you can't. You can only tell him about it or send some pictures and videos of the experience.

You might feel regretful for quitting your career to become a stay-at-home wife and mom (I absolutely hate this term—you don't stay at home. You are a homemaker, one who manages the home). You could be battling jealousy or resentment toward your husband because he's not there. You have house-hunted or apartment-shopped alone because he was overseas playing basketball, and let's be real, he isn't even going to be in that home for more than a few months out of the year anyway. You have packed up your home, moved across country, and then unpacked it all by yourself because a new team picked him up.

You struggle with maintaining a screen-free household but allow kids to use the phone to Face Time daddy. Your phone rings and your daughter screams, "Dad!" but then realizes it's not him and throws a tantrum because she misses her dad, and there's nothing you can do about it. It's the middle of the night in Europe, and he's sleeping or at basketball practice.

Maybe your husband is busy during the time you all normally set aside to talk on the phone. He's had a long, busy day. But he finally calls you before he goes to bed. Only it's just to say hi and goodnight. The worst part is that you have a mouthful of things you want to share and celebrate, but you have to wait until tomorrow to tell him (and by that time you won't be as excited and will probably forget everything you wanted to talk to him about). So you hang up and feel sad because you can't share these big and little things with the one and only person you want to share them with.

If that hasn't happened, maybe your husband calls, but the kids want nothing to do with the phone conversation because they understand he's not physically there with them, and that makes them sad.

You have to strategically discuss important life decisions and issues around game schedules, or he may be in a certain mood and doesn't want to be bothered after a bad practice or rough day at the gym. Perhaps you have to postpone vacation dates and booking flights in advance because you are waiting for playoff games to end, a confirmation from an NBA team, or an overseas contract to finalize.

You have made a Costco haul or stocked up at the grocery store, and you can't carry everything inside the house without taking ten trips back and forth from the car because he's not home to carry it all inside. Not to mention you are exhausted already for braving grocery shopping with all of the kids. You have asked him to help out more around the house, but he's working all the time, and he doesn't know how else he can help. Frustrations arise and the tension in your marriage grows.

You are not the only one feeling this way. You are not alone. If any of this resonates with you, this book is for you. *Help! My Husband is Hardly Home* is about helping you navigate all of the issues that come with raising your family while your husband is constantly working or traveling to provide for the family. To feel fully supported while raising your family, you will come face-to-face with some deeply-rooted trauma and suppressed emotions, which need to be addressed. To do this, you will have to peel back the layers, which are hiding the actual problem and dive deeper into your personal development. For many, this is a challenging and painful inward transformation, usually avoided altogether.

Once you decide to embark on this transformative journey, you will find yourself and the support you need so that the weight of raising your family will be alleviated and distributed. Your husband will pitch in more. You will no longer feel like you are raising your family alone. This process opens the door for many opportunities for personal growth, ways to better serve your family, and most importantly, the ability to show up for yourself.

After your transformation, you will feel capable of juggling it all—wifehood, motherhood, and humanhood. You will no longer lose sleep because you are anticipating tomorrow's overwhelming challenges. It will be easier to wake up in the morning. You will wake up feeling recharged and ready to get your day started, free of unnecessary stress.

You will no longer feel bound and stuck. You will feel free and liberated of the burdens of being the family rock and instead feel empowered because you are the family's rock. You will feel fulfilled, living in your purpose. You will have shed all the feelings of doubt and inadequacy. You will regain control over your life and take back your power. You will become confident in your ability to take care of your husband, hold the house down, raise your family, and maintain your own identity throughout. That is invaluable.

CHAPTER 2

Wife, Mother, but What About Me?

I am happily married to my husband and mama to my beautiful baby, Juniper. I have a private coaching practice where I help women, whose partners travel for work, learn to solo parent with ease.

I am a homemaker who earned two bachelor's degrees and a master's degree. I am also a certified yoga instructor, CEO of the Maurice Ndour Foundation (which is our non-profit foundation), Lightworker, and intuitive life coach. I am a believer of meditation and kundalini energy, breath-led movement enthusiast, vegan foodie, essential oil junkie, crystal lover, and cloth diaper addict. Basically, I am into all things that promote a healthy, whole, and holistic lifestyle. You can find me traveling, exploring the outdoors, hiking, or strolling around a farmer's market—all of the hippie dippie things.

My family instilled strong values, particularly that educational advancement was the key to success. So naturally, I have many academic accolades and accomplishments, but I am not quite using all three of my college degrees in the conventional way you'd think or to the capacity that one would expect.

I played basketball at Miami University (Woo! Love & Honor. Go RedHawks) and earned a bachelor's degree in strategic communications and a bachelor's degree in Spanish in four years. After graduating, I played basketball professionally overseas. After my first year of playing, I missed learning, so I decided to enroll in a master's program in strategic communications at Purdue University online. My plan was to continue to play, and when I completed my master's degree, I would re-evaluate my life, career, goals, desires and dreams.

The following year, I was playing in Mallorca, Spain, waking up next to the beach every morning, meeting so many beautiful people along the way, improving my Spanish, and broadening my global perspective on life. Even though I loved my life, I had decided at the beginning of that season that it would be my last. I felt called to do something else. I felt my purpose had shifted. Although I was making a positive impact in countless lives by playing basketball professionally (role model, philanthropist, and humanitarian), I knew I was put on this earth to touch lives in a different way.

I also had a desire to start a family and settle down. I actually hate that phrase "settle down." I did not settle for my life. I wanted this life I now have. I did not settle with Maurice. He's my soul mate. We chose each other. So I will re-frame that and say I had a desire to create my dream life by meeting my twin flame and growing our family. I yearned to bring life into this world. My heart felt compelled to positively impact the lives of countless individuals (I had no idea at the time that it would be through coaching women or writing a book). Although it was unclear as to how this was going to come about, my intuition told me I was meant to make a difference in the world, that my contributions matter.

Once I made up my mind that it was my last basketball season, it was mid-way through the season when I met Maurice, who was playing professionally for Real Madrid. Also, I tore a few ligaments in my ankle but finished out the season, even though it kept dislocating out of the socket. It became unbearable, and I had surgery after the season was over. It was a four-month recovery, and I easily could have rehabbed and bounced back. It wasn't a career-ending injury, and I could have continued to play. Logically, I should have continued since I was coming off of my best season yet. Nonetheless, I felt deep in my heart that my time as a basketball player was done. And what really sealed the deal was this smooth chocolate man who asked me to move to New York with him. With all the logical reasons to say no—only dating for a little less than a year being one of the many—I followed my heart and moved in with him without hesitation. My family thought I was insane and couldn't understand my decisions, but it was a no-brainer for me—literally, I did not use my brain. I used discernment and heart-coherence instead. (No worries; I'll explain this later.) I packed up my life and drove halfway across the country from Chicago to New York to become a diehard fan for #2 on the New York Knicks.

During that first year living together, I finished up my communications master's degree and became a certified yoga instructor. In hindsight, I realized that during this season with the Knicks, I ultimately lost sight of my own ambitions and just rode Maurice's coattails. I became wrapped up in his dreams, did all I could for him, and left my dreams by the wayside. I spiraled even further away from myself and lost my identity in his. I lost myself. At the time, I really thought I was living the life I had wanted and dreamed of. But when I received all of my wishes, it wasn't what I had expected or what I desired anymore. I knew something had to change. I had to figure out how I fell so far off of my path and how I could get back on track. I am so grateful that it all unfolded and happened the way it did, as it's my divine journey.

Maurice played with the New York Knicks and then the Dallas Mavericks. He then played in Spain with Real Madrid, and then came back stateside with the New York Knicks. He currently plays basketball in Russia for BC Unics Kazan and has been with Unics for the past two seasons, which has brought some stability and security to our chaotic and unpredictable lives, but it's still chaotic and unpredictable, nonetheless.

After the NBA season was over with the Knicks, we were married. We both just knew it was time.

"Yup, this is it."

I am so in love with this man—you all don't even understand. He shines light into my life. He sees the good in everything. He sees a strength in me that I don't always realize is there. He is all the things and gives me all the feels. A month after we married, we became pregnant with Juniper. She is now one year old as I write this, which is just wild to even think about. I am also pregnant.

I am one of those people who love being pregnant. There is no greater feeling than the connection between you and your baby. That bond you develop from the time of conception is something magical. I get chills just thinking about it.

I spent the majority of my first pregnancy alone. Maurice was with me for the first month we knew we were pregnant; so at that point, I was in the last month of the first trimester. We were able to travel and enjoy the offseason. Then, he had to go to Senegal to play for the national team in the World Cup. I was supposed to go too, but the CDC warned pregnant women against traveling there because of an increased Zika risk (*eye roll* I doubt that was even a real thing, but I couldn't have had a peaceful pregnancy knowing that I could have potentially exposed myself and my unborn child to that.) So, we made our first of many tough parenting decisions, and I stayed behind. He was gone for about two months while I remained in New York with no friends or family, The father of my unborn child, my husband, had gone to another continent for work, and I was pregnant. Like hormonal emotional pregnant. All right, cool.

When he returned, we had a nice two months together. It was December, and we were waiting for a team to sign him. In the meantime, we decided to move to Arizona because that's where he trains in the offseason. It just made sense to have our own place conveniently located for offseason training. Scottsdale became our new home base.

Days before the move and our flight to Arizona, he was signed by a team in Russia. The day, the movers came, Maurice signed the contract, and the team booked his flight for the following day. We ended up in the airport together, me heading to Arizona to move in and unpack everything by myself while he headed to Russia to play.

At this point, I was due in two months and was feeling all of the third trimester exhaustion, aches, pains, and stress. I also felt abandoned and alone but also excited because I was able to finally nest and prepare our new home. After I got settled, I felt like I needed love and support, so I went to Chicago where all of my family lives. I ended up staying for three months (one month before baby was due and then two months after).

Luckily, Maurice was able to make it for the birth. My water broke on a Thursday morning, as he was in the air, en route to Chicago from Russia. Juniper was born Friday morning, and Maurice flew back out hours after I was discharged from the hospital on Sunday. Saying "see you later" this time was the hardest one by far. Giving birth and then facing both the greatest and saddest moment alone was one of the hardest things I have ever had to endure. I just wanted to share our love creation for longer than seventy-two hours. But duty calls. Someone's gotta make the donuts.

In all honesty, the pregnancy and giving birth were the easy part. That's the blissful stuff. You come down from that high to realize you're alone, left with a whole human who won't stop eating, keeps you up all night, cries constantly, and requires you to be her whole world. That was extremely difficult to navigate, but here I am, coaching clients on how to get rid of the isolation, overwhelming feelings, and exhaustion of motherhood while their husbands are away.

After my husband's season had ended, he came home, and Juniper was four months old already. She and I had gotten the hang of each other, so we had a good thing going. When he returned, everything changed. Our daily routine was totally different, and we had to find a new jam, one that included my husband. I had to get acclimated to having my husband around. Strange, right?

After a two-month offseason and finally finding our rhythm with three of us at home, it was time for him to leave again for Russia. Alone once again. Thankfully, this time would only be for two months while he got settled. Then we would re-unite and live in Russia for the season. It was so dope having the family together and finally being able to share moments and milestones together. I loved that part, except I still felt the same—alone, unsupported, exhausted, and overwhelmed.

I had raised Juniper for four months while Maurice was gone. Essentially, I was a single mother for four months, without the financial stress—thank God! Even after being together in Russia, I still felt like I was solo parenting. Everything fell on me. I was still dealing with the same stuff I was dealing with stateside—the baby crying, middle of the night waking, early morning waking, rearing, organizing, feeding, cooking, cleaning, shopping, budgeting, bills, tying loose ends back at home, random important paperwork . . . essentially everything. All the while, my husband was enjoying his best life it seemed—playing basketball for a living, traveling the world, staying in hotels, ordering room service, and getting massages and bodywork.

That season in Russia was my breakthrough point. We found out we were pregnant again, and I just couldn't do it all by myself anymore. I was wiped out. I'm talking like the zombie delirious exhaustion. I found myself in a rut. I was drained mentally, physically, and emotionally. Not to mention, Russian winters are no joke. The cold weather, grey skies, lack of sunlight, and somber mood caused me to fall into a deep slump.

It was wearing on me. I didn't like the person and mother I had become. I wasn't fun to be around, and I wasn't smiling like I used to do. My shine had most definitely dulled. I felt like I couldn't keep up with life and was always playing catch up. I also wanted to be in a good mental and emotional state throughout the remainder of my pregnancy for the baby's sake. I was determined to use whatever time I had left before the new baby arrived to get myself in order.

I wanted to get settled stateside, find a midwife, get comfortable with my doula, soak up all the vitamin D I could, build my support system, and get back to doing the things that make me, well, me. I knew I wanted to teach yoga again and rekindle my lost identity. I had this small window to figure out what I wanted for myself and chase my own ambitions before having two babies under two and a husband with a crazy career—there's no telling where he will be playing or what our living situation will be in any given season. In hindsight, I realize the window to figure your dreams and yourself out never closes. But it was in that moment of darkness that a light bulb went off. I knew there was a better way to live life.

You don't have to lose your sense of identity to your children or husband.

You don't have to lose sight of what you truly want in life.

You don't have to live a life where your needs don't exist or aren't met.

You don't have to feel like you're not doing enough.

You don't have to live an unfulfilling life.

You don't have to suffer in silence

You don't have to be exhausted and overwhelmed.

You don't have to feel alone. You are not alone.

So, I created a method to help balance life and receive the support I needed. Since then, my husband has stepped up his game at home, too. He contributes to the household duties and to raising our family to the best of his ability. I've also helped my clients feel like they finally have a handle on things because they are fully supported. With my coaching, they feel like they are much better moms and able to live a much happier and fulfilling life. Who doesn't want that?

The Bottom line is . . . I had to do what made me happy. It turns out, what makes me happy also makes

Maurice happy. I had figured out how to be whole again without him, how to integrate our separate lives when he is home, and how to feel supported in all situations. I figured out how to solve this problem through trial and error, soft-data research, and I also pulled from my own experiences as a professional athlete, which is how I developed this *8-Step Model*.

I also gained a better perspective on things since my dad played basketball professionally in the NBA and overseas for thirteen years, and my older brother began his fourteenth professional basketball season overseas six months ago. He's married with three kids, so my sister-in-law and I appreciate our many similarities. We learn from each other as we venture through this wild journey of raising our families in outside-the-box ways.

It's extremely hard mommy-ing it while being physically alone, sometimes on different continents, and supporting your husband's career choices makes it a thousand times harder. I'm sure you've felt some degree of loneliness, isolation, abandonment, exhaustion, overwhelming thoughts, or resentment. And that's okay. That's why I created this method that works.

Yes, I still have my moments where I feel alone and burdened by it all. I can't always be this radiant, positive gleam of light. Sometimes I ball my eyes out and allow myself to really feel my feelings and release my emotions because I need space to be human, too. Whenever those thoughts creep in or those feelings arise, I always come back to my *8-Step Model* outlined in the next chapter because it works and produces intrinsic and extrinsic results.

Our family dynamic will definitely change as our family continues to grow and as we continue traveling the world, but the same framework can still be applied. I found what works for us as well as many other women. The women I coach are in similar situations and past clients now feel supported throughout their roles and responsibilities within their family unit and most importantly, within themselves.

Chapter 3

Getting Started

M y *8-Step Model* begins as you check in with yourself. The complete steps are as follows:

- Take inventory of your unique family situation. Acknowledging your situation gives you a point of reference so that you have a baseline for where you are.

- Find your triggers, making you more aware, less reactive, and more compassionate in stressful situations.

- Say goodbye. Look back to see what you've overcome throughout your journey and celebrate the victories (big and small) along the way.

- Say hello to yourself and know your own beauty. Redefine yourself and reclaim your identity. This step ignites this monumental shift in your life, which is empowering. You will feel like an actual human again and not just a lost soul in your role as a wife or mother.
- Mother yourself.
- See things through your husband's perspective, giving you a widened, more empathetic view toward him and your entire family dynamic.
- Find your normalcy, regardless of the circumstances, making you well equipped to manage the household and family when he's around and when he's away.
- Build your support system, which will uplift you and encourage you along the way.

It is extremely beneficial for you to follow the framework in the outlined order. Each subsequent step builds on the previous. If you go through the framework to solve your problem but still have trouble in a certain area, I would recommend going back to the specific step you are stuck on and work through the block. The steps are simple and logical, but the hard part is actually actioning the steps. That's where my coaching can be very helpful and accelerate the process. You will be required to turn inward and peel back the layers to expose the root issue and revisit trauma you've been avoiding. This can be a painfully hard process, but it's worth it.

The framework is not only an *8-Step* guide to feeling supported while raising your family, but it will also take you on a spiritual journey to rediscover your identity, which ultimately allows you to better serve your family. You will learn how to get reacquainted with yourself, accepting all facets, which in turn makes you a better mother, wife, and human being. Along the way, you will understand from where any resentment stems, the trick to coping with your husband's absence, the secret to getting your husband to help out more, the key to balancing the family's daily routine with his cameos, and the easiest way to improve your overall mood.

CHAPTER 4

Take Inventory of Your Unique Family Situation

Step 1: Acknowledge Your Situation

It's normal to want to be the best wife you can be to your husband and the best mother you can be to your children. For me, I know my most important role is wife. My next most important role is mother to my babies. I am a very competitive, determined, passion-driven individual, so it's in my nature to carry out those duties to the best of my ability. That is what propelled me to play basketball professionally, and although I retired, why would I be any different now? I am always striving to be the best and do my best. Even though I often feel like what I am doing is not nearly enough, I still try to do everything in my power to support my husband and take on the responsibility of raising my family, and I attribute that to the caregiver archetype in me.

The caregiver archetype is most dominant in women, and especially mothers. An archetype is a theme or a general characteristic we all embody to some degree. It is a recurrent symbol that appears in our behavior and psychological being. Some people have more of one archetype readily visible than others, but each of us encompasses all twelve archetypes. It's as simple as dialing in to that version of you, much like turning on a radio station or changing the channel on the TV.

The caregiver archetype is an energy that lives in the collective unconscious. The caregiver is a representation of you and the role you most prominently play every day. The caregiver loves unconditionally and is quick to forgive. It is the caregiver's deepest desire to protect others, care for others, and to serve others. The caregiver loves unconditionally, shows compassion, and lives generously. She is the ultimate selfless woman.

Sound familiar? As a caregiver, you constantly give yourself to your husband and kids as you are serving them. You generally tend to put the needs of others before your own and the number one priority is supporting them. I was constantly concerned with my husband's needs and desires before my own, and I always thought about Juniper before myself. Countless times, I had forgotten to eat or realized in the evening that I had not eaten all day. I forgot to eat so many times because I was making sure my family was fed. It's crazy right? But I know I am not the only one. On top of that, I put my dreams and ambitions on hold in order to raise my family—able to uproot and move to whatever city Maurice was playing in that time.

You most likely feel as if you aren't doing enough and have become exhausted from doing what you are currently doing while trying to do more. Whatever you want done, it seems like there aren't enough hours in the day to get it all done or that you just aren't capable of completing it yourself. I, too, felt like I wasn't doing my job well enough. It was so frustrating, stressful, and upsetting to think that I was lacking something or not enough for my family.

Juniper and I had our morning routine and, in addition to cooking two or three times a day, I would also make snacks for my husband to take with him for the five to six hours he spent at the gym. Disclaimer: I am a vegan who could live off of smoothies, fresh juice, and vegetable stir-fry, and Maurice is a seafood and fish lover. He appreciates good food, but that means I am cooking two different meals between one to three times per day, just about every day. Oh, and here's the kicker: I am not a master chef, nor do I really enjoy cooking. So imagine how stressful this was for me. Honestly, who enjoys cooking food they can't even taste? I do, though, enjoy baking, and I like to cook my favorite dishes. But I cook because it means a lot for Maurice to come home from practice and able to smell a good home-cooked meal and see his wife "cheffing" it up in the kitchen. Believe me, I wouldn't spend so much time in the kitchen, but cooking is an act of service and his favorite way to receive love. I relish in being able to put a hot meal on the table for my husband and get instant satisfaction because he is smashing. So of course, I am going to show him love. I just had to find a way to do it so that it didn't weigh me down or make me so stressed out.

I am all for new age ways of marriage where both partners share equal responsibilities, and I am a firm believer that your marriage gets to look like however you want it to look. Being a wife can mean something totally different to me than it does to someone else. But for me, I lie somewhere in the middle of the traditional-new age spectrum, leaning toward more traditional roles. I love staying home to raise my family and take care of my husband, but on the other hand, I am not his mother. I do believe that men were created for and are better suited to do certain things than women and women were created to do certain things more efficiently and better than men. Men and women were not created equally (that's not to say that we shouldn't have equal rights and pay). We complement each other. I, personally, love that Maurice is the breadwinner and that I get the opportunity to stay at home with our babies and hold down the house. But I also believe that he can pick up after himself, tidy up the house, run errands, parent and spend time with our kids (see how I didn't say watch the kids), and I can bring home some dollars too.

In addition to the whole cooking situation, I still take care of the mounds of laundry, cleaning, grocery shopping with a baby (OMG, the struggle of a greedy one-year-old), and then haul the grocery bags and baby up the stairs to the apartment in one trip from the parking garage. Normally, he's not home to help me take in groceries, so I wrap Juniper on me (with a woven wrap or a buckle carrier), and we lug it all inside.

Literally, you name it, we women can be it. Wife, mama, secretary, accountant, assistant, housekeeper, chef, support system, business partner, rock, the glue that holds everything together. That's all you!

Ultimately, that life outlined above is not sustainable in the long-term. I know I am the "perfect" wife in spurts. I get everything under control, and I am on top of everything for a short stint here and there. I will get into the swing of things—planning out meals for the week, writing my grocery list, actually sticking to the grocery list, cooking with a grumpelstiltskin wrapped on my back, having the house clean and organized, spending quality time with Juniper, engaging in educational and sensory play, and trying to look halfway decent. Then when he leaves, I let it all go because it feels like I can't breathe. I can only maintain that lifestyle for so long until it all unravels, and I'm left worn out. This is when I realized I needed a helping hand.

Don't even get me started on game days. The most stressful days of all. These days are when his performance matters most. This is when my performance matters most. I have to be on it. Planned breakfast, pack snacks for the gym to eat before treatment and shoot around, have food ready for when he comes home from shoot around, and fix him a snack before he leaves for the game. After he leaves for the game, that's when I have twenty minutes to just sit. Then, it's getting Juniper and myself ready to go to the game and getting out the door on time. Stressful is all I can say. And sitting through the games with a busybody who won't sit still is another story. I miss the entire game because I am trying to contain my daughter the whole time. Thank God we were in a big city this year, which meant restaurants were open after late games, so we usually went out to eat with his teammates and their families or ordered in.

Aside from normal mom struggles, we have to deal with things that come with marrying a professional athlete.

A client of mine had to move alone because of a mid-season NBA trade and again at the end of the season because of free agency. At the end of the season, she had to stay behind to pack up the entire house and move halfway across the country while her husband had to report to training immediately. She's also had to deal with multiple mid-season trades, but with the most recent trade, she did not end up moving with her husband. He was going to be a free agent at the end of the season, and if she packed up shop and moved with him, they essentially would be moving again at the end of the season in four months when he signed somewhere else. Not worth it. So, they chose to keep their home, and she and their eighteen-month-old would commute from their home base to her husband's new team, spending two weeks in each city. Talk about trying to find a rhythm. The sacrifices she's made and the lengths she continues to go to support her husband's dreams while keeping her family together is so admirable. I witnessed her strength and resilience through eleven moves in a six-year span. She is one beautiful, strong mama who again and again finds what she feels is right for her family.

Similarly, Maurice and I moved to Arizona because the season with the New York Knicks ended. It was looking like he would end up playing basketball overseas the following season, and we wanted to have a home base in the place he typically trains in the offseason. So, we had scheduled the movers, shipped the cars, and booked flights for Arizona. We packed up our place in New York—let's be real, I pretty much did the packing (mind you, I was in my third trimester with Juniper at the time). The day the movers were coming, Maurice got a call, and he signed to play for Unics in Kazan, Russia. That evening, the team sent his plane ticket, and he had to leave for Russia the next day, which was the same day we were supposed to move out to Arizona. I was in disbelief. It hit me that I would be moving across country, unpacking, and organizing our new place by myself two months before my due date. This was not real life (oh but it was!). It wasn't the smoothest move since the movers lost some of our things and broke about half of our plates, bowls, and cups. But you know what? I did it. I got it done and had fun doing it. I made our cozy home.

The things we do for our families and the lengths we go to support our husbands are endless. This past season, I traveled for almost a full day to get from

Scottsdale, Arizona to Kazan, Russia with Juniper. She was seven or eight months old at the time. It was just her and me. We flew out of Phoenix to San Francisco. For whatever reason, we had to claim our bags and re-check them. We had three checked bags because I was bringing a ton of things Maurice had forgotten, along with Juniper's things, and I barely had room for a few outfits for myself. I also had the diaper bag filled with the essentials—changes of clothes for both of us, diapers, wipes, essential oils for travel, a few small toys, my computer, and important documents we might need to reference while overseas. We ran through the airport trying to make a quick connection in San Francisco. I wrapped Juniper on my front with my Reclaim Woven wrap, I slung Maurice's djembe drum on my back, and rolled three giant suitcases to the security checkpoint to recheck. For most people, their anxiety would have been at one hundred on a scale to one hundred, but I knew there was no need to stress about it. I knew I had everything under control. From there, we flew thirteen hours to Turkey and had a five-hour layover, and then we flew four hours to Kazan, the final destination. I was wiped out after that trip, but I knew how much it meant to Maurice to have his family out there and how much I wanted to support him through his professional basketball career. Clearly, I must love him for me to do the crazy things I do for him.

I share these stories to show you that it's okay to acknowledge and take inventory of your situation. It's completely normal to have many less than ideal circumstances thrown your way. However, it's not okay to complain constantly. Complaining is essentially non-acceptance of what is happening. Complaining carries an unconscious negative charge, and it turns you into the victim. Kelsey Domiana is not a victim. Neither are you. I don't want to complain about my husband or debate about how hard my life is. That's not a debate I want to win or even have. You shouldn't either. It's not a badge of honor or something to be proud of. I am still guilty of complaining at times because, let's face it, I am not perfect. They key is to be aware of when we do complain and how we respond to the situation.

When you realize what complaining actually is and how heavy complaining really is, you will make a conscious effort to not complain. Re-wire your way of thinking and perception around complaining. You are responsible for how you feel and ultimately what you do to change the outcome of the situation. See, when you complain, seldom do you change your behavior or actions. You just like to talk about all of the things that are hard, wrong, annoying, unfair, and imbalanced. Maybe you even like the attention of the sympathy you receive when you complain.

You have the ability to control the "controllables," I like to say. You get to control what you can control. You can control how you respond, and the power lies in how you respond. Therefore, the power is in your control. The power lies in you.

As much as it may sound like I dread my life or how hard I think I have it, it is all just to paint the picture of how I used to view it. The bottom line is, I love my life, I have a wonderful husband, and I wouldn't want to do life with anyone else other than Maurice. I wouldn't want him to stop playing the game he loves to be home with the family. Yes, it's a lot for one person to take on, but that's where finding ways for Maurice to contribute and finding creative solutions really helps me out a ton.

My situation is uncommon and unique. It is specific to Maurice and me. I am a professional basketball player turned pregnant homemaker, mother, and life coach, and Maurice is a professional basketball player. The fact that sometimes I don't see my husband for months at a time can be devastating to many couples, but it's our norm. The longest we have been apart was four months for a couple of times. One of those stints was recent, when we came home from Russia pregnant and with an eleven-month-old. The other was just days after I gave birth to our sweet Juni Love. Most wives would be bitter and angry, and they would complain about how unfair the circumstances were—having to heal physically, psychologically, emotionally, and spiritually from a traumatic birth experience, take care of a whole fresh human, and take care of herself sans husband. But I have learned to check the negativity and complaining at the door.

Likewise, your situation is unique and is specific to you and your partner. Your husband can only control his job to a certain extent, and you can't change the situation by complaining. All you can do is acknowledge what is, roll with it, and make it work somehow.

You need to stop playing the victim of your circumstances, accept your situation, and move forward to find a new rhythm of life.

Your responsibility is your response-ability (response-ability = ability to respond). The stress comes from your lack of response-ability, not the actual situation. Adjust the way in which you respond. For example, change your thoughts and then attitude, and the extra anxiety, stress, and overwhelm go away. When you change how you respond, you are no longer reactive, but aware and proactive.

Yes, you are at home with the kids so most of the time, the weight will all fall on you. Although it may appear unequal on the surface, you can still have an equal partnership.

Your role in your family is to be the rock. You are the congealing agent that holds everyone and everything together. You are the special sauce that makes the vegan burger bang! You are the gatekeeper of information and the concierge of the household. If you waver or stop playing your roles, it all crumbles down. That realization can be daunting and heavy, right? It all falls on you. It doesn't seem like it's fair. But, on the flip side, it is also empowering. You have the power and influence to create whatever dynamic you choose. You have the ability to make your strange family dynamic work. You can design it to look like whatever you want it to look like.

Of course, my husband has things he's responsible for as well. This all wouldn't be possible if he didn't contribute around the house, work relentlessly, and put his physical wellbeing on the line every day to provide for us. Each day I wake up and serve my family to the best of my ability. My husband does the same. That's how our family unit works.

Your structure and routines may look different than mine, but that's the beauty of it. Your family structure gets to look however you want it to look. The first step to creating that family dynamic, that desire to excel, is to acknowledge your situation. As long as you acknowledge your current situation and work on your response-ability, you can see what you can improve upon and change. It will be so much easier to pinpoint what's been working for you and what hasn't been working with this benchmark.

CHAPTER 5:

Discover What Bates You

Step 2: Find Your Triggers

Do you ever vent to the same people over and over again but grow more frustrated than before because they don't really understand what you're going through? Or worse, they don't know what to tell you because they don't know to fix things. Are you annoyed because your husband doesn't actually see all that you really do?

Your marriage suffers and you and your husband drift further and further apart because of these toxic thoughts. I have to admit, sometimes when I used to think about all of the responsibilities that fall on me, I used to feel bothered by my husband for even the littlest things he'd do, or not do. Do you feel bothered by little things too? I bet you desperately need some support in your life.

By knowing when you are triggered, you can take a step back and become more aware of them. Then you can figure out why you are feeling the way you do. These feelings and emotions are surfacing for a reason, and you have to figure out why.

For example, you are so frustrated by your husband's lack of contribution around the house and with the family, it manifests as an argument over something little. When that happens, it's helpful to ask yourself what is actually bothering you and why you are feeling this way. Normally, the action that caused the feelings to surface is a trigger releasing big emotions. Those emotions blur how you respond to the situation and you react irrationally—small, nitpicky fights or an all-out blow up. It's time for you to look inward and decipher where it all stems from.

Another helpful technique is to differentiate between what is actually true and what is just story you tell yourself. We always tell ourselves stories we believe are true, but there is a truer reality that better serves you.

You may feel triggered by the following emotions:

Regret

During your most stressful days or in the middle of the night feedings when craziness is at an all time high, you have most likely felt regretful to a certain degree. You have to ask yourself why you feel regret or what is it that you regret. For most, it's that we regret giving up our careers, consequently losing our old identities. Perhaps you made the decision to stop working to start or raise your family. I chose to retire from playing basketball and pursue other avenues in my life. It was my decision to stop working, get married, and start a family because at the time, that was what I wanted. Who knows how many more championships I could have won, what other accolades I could have racked up, what other countries I could have played in, or for how many more years my body could withstand the constant pounding? When these regret-filled questions would surface, I felt guilty and selfish for thinking this way.

When regret creeps in, it doesn't mean you don't love your husband, marriage, or kids. It just means that all of this bottled up emotion was festering for too long without an outlet. You haven't dealt with it at its very core. It now surfaces through various nitpicky fights or disagreements and creates disconnect between you and your husband and kids. Most importantly, you have to find the root cause of it all—your lost identity.

You were once a self-sufficient woman with her own life, goals, career, and income who now relies on her husband to provide for her. Once I had my marriage and family, I felt like giving up my career really meant I had to rely on Maurice, and I was required to surrender my independence only to have my children become solely reliant on me. But that doesn't have to be your truth. You are still an independent, self-sufficient, whole woman who willingly chose to embark on a new journey. You see how this statement is truer?

Insecurity

Something triggers your insecurity, and you get mad about something that happened days ago that isn't even the issue at hand. You may feel a rush of negative emotions when your husband goes out with his teammates in a different city after an away game. He is out with the guys and you know there are thirsty women throwing themselves at him. Your mind spirals out of control, and you wonder if you think you are enough. You may think it is impossible for him to resist temptation when he has women at his disposal and has such convenient access all the time. You feel like you lack something and question if you are enough.

This is when you have to dig deep and find that truer statement. You are worthy and enough because you are you. You were not created to be like anyone else. There is no one on this planet who is you, and that is something to be celebrated. You are exactly who you are meant to be. Do you see how much truer those statements are rather than the story you tell yourself?

Choose to no longer operate out of fear and lack. Instead choose abundance. Everything that is for you will always be for you.

Jealousy

The flip side to insecurity is jealousy. He's receiving all of this unwarranted (maybe it's sometimes warranted) attention from the opposite sex, but you aren't. He is out at a team appearance, a lounge eating, or the club with the guys receiving attention from women, meanwhile you are grocery shopping and can't get a man's attention to help you carry your bags out to the car or even just hold the door open. You could be at home waiting up for him, or you might be in a different time zone scraping your screaming child off of the floor at Target. Either way, you are not receiving the much desired and needed attention from the opposite sex like your husband is constantly experiencing. That's where you need to look within and give yourself some much-needed attention.

Stress

You probably feel the stress creep in when you look at the way your house is disorganized—toys sprawled out everywhere, consuming the entire living room, dishes in the sink, crumbs covering the floor, laundry piled high, and stacks of papers everywhere. You definitely feel stressed when you need only five more minutes to finish making lunch, but your hangry, whining toddler is yanking on your pants, and it's the only time your husband is free to talk before he goes to bed in Europe.

How about when your husband leaves his plate on the table after a meal or puts a dirty dish in your perfectly clean, empty sink when he is home. I'm sure it drives you nuts. You know he just saw you cook dinner and then watched you wash all of the dishes, dry them, and put them away. It's as if you finally provided some order against the chaos, and then he adds right back to it.

I couldn't stand it when Maurice would go out after a home game with his teammates, and I'd be at home trying to sleep but not really able to sleep because I had to know that he came home safely. And let's be real. He wakes me up anyway when I hear him walk in the door or when he crawls into the bed. So, my whole sleep cycle is disrupted, and now I'm already tired for tomorrow before it's even tomorrow. Ugh. Sleep deprived stress is no joke.

Or your husband is home for a few days and says he will pick up the groceries but accidentally falls asleep on the couch instead. Groceries had been taken off your to-do list but now unexpectedly, they have been added back on. Cue the frantic panic.

Essentially, it all boils down to two things:

Envy

Envy, the desire to have what someone else has, is one of the main roots of triggers. You envy your husband's unchanged life. It appears that his life has hardly changed, but your life had been flipped upside down. The regret, insecurity, and jealousy make you envious of his consistent life.

My husband was staying up late and sleeping in, but I did not have that luxury anymore. It was annoying, and I envied him for being able to sleep.

Excuse me, you mean to tell me I have to stay in with Juniper while you go out with the guys? I can't go so, "No, you shouldn't even want to go," type of thing. I also feel very envious during pregnancy. Maurice is able to go out and drink, and I can't. And it's strange because normally, unpregnant Kelsey Domiana doesn't even like to go out or drink. *Because I can't, you shouldn't even want to.* My thought process was simple.

But the other side is that just because you are not able to drink or go out doesn't mean he has to stay in or not drink.

Either way, it feels like you two are living two separate lives, even on different continents sometimes. It's like you give into everybody but given nothing in return, except depletion and exhaustion.

He is able to FaceTime us at home when it's convenient for him, but I can't just press the red button to hang up and make it all go away like he can.

Essentially, the envy stems from his freedom to move around when he pleases, not the fact that he goes out with the guys. Do you, man! The trust factor isn't the issue in this case.

You most definitely feel envious that he has a life outside of you, but your life only revolves around him and your kids. He is able to engage in adult conversation when he goes to work and with friends. When you are at "work" you are talking to little humans who barely say mama or only say mama. It can make you go crazy!

Another way my life has changed tremendously and his hasn't is that I cannot shower or use the bathroom in peace anymore—luxuries I once took for granted. I bet your husband can still use the bathroom in private. I'm sure he can easily have ten minutes of uninterrupted leisure toilet time. Talk about envy. I have to admit though, I was petty once upon a time, and I used to crack the door open so that Juniper could crawl or walk inside the bathroom when he was in there, or I would even just pick her up and put her in the bathroom just so he could have a taste of what a changed life feels like. I needed that ten-minute break. I was determined to make him feel what I felt and experience the things he didn't have to experience because he was hardly home. I see now that there was a much better way to get my point across to him. Oops! Trial and error, right? You live and you learn.

He gets to travel the world, stay in hotels, and Face-Time us at the end of his day when it is convenient for him or fits in with his schedule. To you, it may feel like your husband is living the good life, meanwhile you're at home all day holding down the fort and taking care of a fussy, teething, clingy baby, trying to remember if you brushed your teeth or ate at all that day. It's annoying, and you have every right to feel envious.

You couldn't be living two more different lives sometimes. When you get sick, the world doesn't stop. No one takes care of you, and you still have to carry out the same responsibilities as normal, (You might skip cooking. Yay!) It's wild because it took two to make a baby, but it's just the woman who raises one? Hmm. Not cool. As a homemaker and mom, you get no breaks or time off. The fact that your husband gets to resume his normal life, go to work every day, come home, and kick it, fills you with envy while you are worrying about literally everything else.

You don't have to feel that way. You can take breaks, have a social life, and find your new normalcy, one that actually feels good.

Inadequacy

The other main root of triggers is inadequacy. You never feel you are doing enough or that you are enough. I somehow drop the ball, forget something on the to-do list, or burn the dinner I worked so hard on preparing (I am almost too good at doing this!). You feel like you aren't capable of getting it all done. That added stress makes you feel even more overwhelmed and as a result, you feel inadequate.

During both of my pregnancies, while going through all the hormonal, physiological, psychological, and spiritual transformations, Maurice was either away for months at a time, either in Senegal playing with the National Team or in Russia finishing out the rest of the season. Being pregnant is hard enough, but when you add in guest appearances by Maurice—only days at a time or seeing him for a couple months on and then a couple months off, it's taxing. I am the one going through all of the changes, and all I want is for him to be here with me, experiencing all the things with me (the nausea, the two and three-day-long migraines, the extreme fatigue, the butterflies and kicks, the doctor's appointments, the fear, the excitement, and the joy). Being pregnant, emotional, and alone has had to be the hardest and greatest thing I did. And yet, here I am again! Pregnant and stateside while my husband is overseas and working. I remember crying one time when he was home. I poured my entire heart and soul out to him only to follow it up by asking him if he was doing okay with this whole pregnancy thing and how can I better serve him. I felt inadequate because I wasn't doing everything I was doing before. I didn't feel like I was doing enough at the time because I was doing less around the house. Wild right? Of course, I was doing enough. I was doing more than enough. I am growing life, doing inner healing work, resting, eating healthy, being the best version of myself, and showing up for my family and myself. What else could he have asked for? What else could I have asked from myself? What else could I have done? Nothing. Because I am adequate . . . more than adequate. And you are too. What you are doing is enough.

You wear all the hats and think about the things that he would never think about. You make sure the house is taken care of—bills, expenses, taxes, appointments, car maintenance, shopping, cooking, cleaning, babies, growing life, and all those little never-ending things on that to-do list. I am almost positive I am missing more of the hats you wear, but you get the point. You make sure your kids are fed, clothed, and loved. That's all you. So there's no reason to feel inadequate.

All of those feelings listed above (regret, insecurity, jealousy, stress) boil down to your envy toward him and the inadequacy you feel within yourself, which leads you to resent him. I resented the fact his life didn't change. I resented that it made me feel inadequate. This will ultimately take a toll on your marriage, how you interact with your kids, and how you view yourself. You are in no way, shape, or form your highest self or best version of you when you feel resentment toward your man.

These feelings will resurface every now and then. Like I said before, I am not perfect, but I am cognizant of when they do. I understand what triggers the resentment and have found the root of my triggers.

You have to use your voice, learn to love without condition, talk without bad intention, give without any reason, and most of all, care for people without any expectation.

I used to project my feelings onto Maurice and pick fights when I would get triggered, But I have to remind myself that these emotions are surfacing for a reason. You can learn from your triggers. They keep showing up because you haven't learned the lesson yet. Remind yourself that it is you and your husband versus the problem, not your husband versus you. Your husband is not the problem. The problem is the problem, and you will solve that problem together. Know your triggers so that you can create awareness and be more compassionate in your relationships.

I want to clarify that I am not publicly badmouthing my husband. I am being honest, transparent, and vulnerable while sharing with you the struggles that no one wants to talk about publicly. I am not saying Maurice is a bad husband or negligent father. He is actually a caring and loving husband and a dope dad. He is doing what he knows how to do to the best of his ability, as am I. I am sharing what works for us (and my clients) with the hope that it will help you, too.

The lack of his contributions around the house and raising our family is frustrating and overwhelming at times, but at the end of the day, our unconventional situation works for us. He will not be playing basketball professionally forever. I'm sure after he retires, he will still be working and traveling to some capacity. So in the meantime, we will enjoy this ride while it lasts and continue to use my *8-Step Model* to thrive through it all.

To paraphrase Elizabeth Gilbert's famous lines on soul mates, I have realized that throughout our journey together Maurice is a mirror. Your husband shows you everything that is holding you back. He is the person who draws attention to the places you need healing the most. He tears down the barriers you have built. He shakes and wakes you up. His purpose is to purge you of your ego so that you can shed those layers and break your heart open, permitting new light to enter. Your life as you once knew it feels like it's in shambles whereas you have no choice but to awaken and transform your life.

Maurice has done all of that from the day that I met him. He has challenged me. I have never been challenged by anyone so much before. He challenges the conventional way of thinking, doing, and being, and he has expanded my perspective on so many things. He came into my life and shook everything up. The very things that attracted me to him also were the things that I needed to call attention to within myself. He exposed so many qualities I knew existed within but needed him as my mirror to see them in myself clearly. Maurice has awakened my soul and transformed my life for the better.

Chapter 6:

Look Back and Celebrate

Step 3: Say Goodbye to the Old You

Your entire world revolves around your family. You think your sole duty is raising your family. Your family is your life. Everything you do and every decision you make is with your husband and your babes in mind. You are most definitely so wrapped up in him that you've lost yourself.

I didn't realize just how much I had lost myself in my husband and his career until I felt so overwhelmed and empty inside. I forgot who I was and made decisions solely focused on being everything Maurice needed me to be. When in reality, Maurice needed me to just be me—my whole self.

Prior to starting my family, I was self-sufficient, making my own money and living my own life. I was an independent, strong woman making a way for herself, just like my mom exemplified. I was educated with two bachelor's degrees, a master's degree, a solid basketball career, and yoga certification. But I wanted to drop everything to support Maurice and his career. Shortly after, I had Juniper and ended up losing myself even more. It is hard to accept that you are independent yet reliant on your partner and synergistically working together.

Do you struggle to answer this simple question: "Who am I?" It sounds fairly easy to answer, right? But it can be the most complex, loaded question for someone who has lost her identity to her family. Think about how you feel when someone asks you, "What are you doing with your life?" Or, "So . . . what do you do now?" Those words sting deep in your soul.

In order to answer these questions, it's necessary to mourn the woman you once were and the person you used to be. You also must heal the past trauma you experienced in order to let go and move forward. You also can't forget to celebrate your triumphant journey and victories along the way.

Especially in western society, we seldom acknowledge motherhood as a rite of passage. Motherhood is typically seen as something that just happens suddenly.

There is no preparation for the emotional, psychological, and physical changes you will experience before, during, and—especially—after. But viewing motherhood as a rite of passage is an integral part of stepping forward into that role and closing past chapters of your life and the woman you once were. It is very hard to let go of the image and the woman you were before you had kids, but it is so necessary to continue to forge ahead. You have to create space by clearing out the old, heavy, stagnant, and stale energy. This makes room to welcome the new, light, and fresh you. You must close the chapter of your old version of what independence means to you, your pre-motherhood self, and sometimes your career to be able to write the rest of the book, your story.

Conceiving, pregnancy, birthing, and postpartum took me through a series of life and death cycles. I am aware of the old parts of me that have died as well as the parts within me that have birthed and rebirthed. This entire process has been a constant flow and continuum of evolution and awakening. Throughout the entire transition into motherhood, I died many times but was also reborn again and again. After each stage—conception, pregnancy, birthing, and postpartum—I died, but the death propelled me into the subsequent stage, born again. After conception, I shed the woman I once was but welcomed the seed that would grow in my womb and the woman who was capable of growing life. Once pregnancy was over, I died as I began the birthing process as a new woman and mother. After surrendering to birth, I died and was reborn again as I embarked on my unprepared postpartum journey. And again, I mourned as I navigated through a dark postpartum period and experienced rebirth as that fourth trimester ended, and I entered into motherhood fully. This process repeats each time you have kids as you rebirth into motherhood and womanhood and experience it in its entirety. Shedding and growing is inevitable. This death-rebirth cycle doesn't have to be a sad thing either. It's a celebration and a welcoming with an open heart to what is divinely ordered for you.

You continue to rise. You transform into an ascending divine warrior queen. During this journey into motherhood, you navigate fear, doubt, isolation, loneliness, confusion, challenges, acceptance, and surrender. In the end, you give birth to a new ancestor, your sweet little baby. "Again and again, motherhood demands that we break through our limitations, that we split our hearts open to make room for something that may be more than we thought we could bear. In that sense, the labor which we give birth is simply a rehearsal for something we mothers must do over and over: turn ourselves inside out, and then let go." as Susan Piver , a writer and meditation teacher, says.

In the end, I gave birth to a brand new me. Rebirth of my own soul. I have a deepened understanding of myself through conscious growth, self-development, and self-awareness. There is wisdom that has been undoubtedly gained after passing through the portal.

It is time to say goodbye to the woman you used to be and welcome the woman you are right now in this moment.

One way to do this is to make an exhaustive list of your accomplishments. It can range from the little things—for example, being cavity-free for over six years—to something colossal, such as setting a precedent at Miami University for being the first full-scholarship student-athlete who played a two-semester sport to study abroad for the entire summer at the university's expense. (No I'm not bragging. I am just super proud of myself, as you should be of your colossal accomplishments, too.) It doesn't matter how small or big the achievements may seem, write them all out. I dare you to tell me you don't feel good about yourself after reading that entire list. This exercise shows you just how far you've come and all of the obstacles you've overcome. So celebrate yourself and celebrate your journey. This exercise also shows you that you are enough, you are capable, and you are a beautiful being whose contribution matters in this world!

This exercise also creates a container that gives you permission to move forward from the woman you used to be. If you stay the same, it will be nearly impossible to add to your running list of accomplishments. If you stay the same, it will be impossible to fully step into your new roles in life and thrive as a mother, wife, and woman. You have the permission to close those past chapters of your life to create space for you to become who you are meant to be. You have permission to add to that list of accomplishments. You cannot dwell in the past and expect to heal. We heal the past by living fully present. Close your eyes to old ends and open your heart to new beginnings.

Chapter 7:

Accept Yourself and Know Your Own Beauty

Step 4: Say Hello, Beautiful

Shifting

Now that you have mourned the woman you once were, it is time for shifting. Mourning creates an opportunity for a shift in perspective, shifting your mindset into a positive point of view. This doesn't mean you are upbeat and happy all the time. It just means you choose to look at things from an elevated perspective. Instead of seeing the fault, find the opportunity, goodness or blessing in the situation. Instead of asking yourself why this is happening to you, ask yourself why this is happening for you. Instead of saying you have to do something, think of it as you have an opportunity to do something. Remember, acting as a victim carries an unconscious negative charge. This is essentially counterproductive to the positive perspective you just consciously created. Ask yourself, "What is this trying to teach me?" Or, "What can I take away from this situation?" Find the opportunity in every obstacle and situation. This simple shift in your outlook will miraculously change things for you.

Heart Coherence

Next, you must get super heart coherent. Heart coherence is a scientific concept called heart math. It essentially conceptualizes what we know to be true spiritually. Shift into a heart coherent state, and the heart and the brain work synergistically to produce a higher vibration and more intuitive access and flow. When you become heart coherent, you allow intuitive suggestions to become priority over choices from the ego. The spiritual heart has an intuitive intelligence and energetic connection to mind and brain. You gain increased access to your heart's intuitive guidance as you practice tuning inward. Produce synergy and heightened intuition by tapping into your heart. Heart coherence not only benefits you, but it benefits the people around you, as well as animals and the environment by producing higher outcomes. A simpler way to explain heart coherence is the tapping into your heart to strengthen your intuition to guide you and produce a higher vibration.

Essentially, when you become heart coherent, you find your purpose and what you are called to do. This means you have to tune into source to listen to your heart's desires. Source can mean whatever you want it to mean: God, the universe, Jah, Most High, within, heart, yourself, or a combination of these.

To get heart coherent, you will first need to get grounded. Place your feet on the floor, walk outside barefoot, stick your feet in the dirt or grass, rub your palms together like you're starting a fire, place your hands on your chest, close your eyes, or take deep belly breaths. These are all easy ways to get grounded just about anywhere, especially for a busy mom. Once you are grounded, sit up tall, place your feet flat on the ground, and close your eyes. It's heart coherence time. It doesn't have to be for a long. Just a minute or two. During this time that you are getting heart coherent, call your attention back inward toward your body, give yourself gratitude, ask for clarity on what your heart desires, and ask for guidance to walk in your purpose.

You will notice that when you are heart coherent your intuition grows stronger, gets louder, and leads you. You will learn to listen and trust your gut over time, rather than rely on others for their advice or guidance. Your instincts and feelings are there to tell you how close or far off you are from what's meant for you. Other people can't help you with that. I mean, I can help you with strategies and exercises to strengthen your intuition and heart coherence, but ultimately, your intuition is for you. Your intuition is guiding you step-by-step saying, "Yes this feels right. Do more of this." That is called energetic resonance. If it's "Nah, that feels off," stay away from that. That is called energetic dissonance. As you continue to practice heart coherence, your internal compass will lead the way, and it will become very hard to ignore your intuition.

It's time to find your purpose through heart coherence now that you know how to dial into it. Finding your own life apart from your kids and husband is also a major part of the reclaiming process. Your life might include a hobby, time with friends, exercise, a side-hustle, a new business, a job, or even a full-fledged career. No matter what it is, finding and living in your purpose is a huge part of regaining your own identity separate from your roles as a wife and mother.

Your intuition is fixed upon your purpose. It will subtly let you know when you are on track and when you are falling astray. So, listen to it. You'll often find that problems occur when you don't trust your intuition or listen to your gut. You will experience overwhelm, stress, disconnect, discomfort, or disease. On the contrary, when you trust your intuition, synchronicity will become very evident. Ever notice how you think about someone, and minutes later they call or text you? Or when you don't want something bad to happen but then it happens? Or you see sequences of numbers like 4:44 or 1:11 or 11:11? Eventually, you will stop calling them coincidences and realize how powerful you are. Synchronicities are simple nudges from the universe and signs from the Most High that you are heart coherent and on the right path.

"To make the right choices in life, you have to get in touch with your soul. To do this, you need to experience solitude, which most people are afraid of because in the silence you hear the truth and know solutions," says Deepak Chopra. Getting heart coherent will help grow your maternal instincts and help you make decisions that are best for your family because the solution is inside of you. You won't have to look for outside validation or reassurance anymore because you know deep in your heart that your intuition is leading you, and it will never steer you astray.

Meditation

Daily meditation is something that has helped me tremendously whenever I have felt overwhelmed, stressed, afraid, angry, jealous, regretful, resentful, or overly exhausted to the point of breaking down in tears—basically any and all of the feels. I even meditate when I am happy and excited to heighten the bliss. I simply re-center, draw consciousness back within myself, become really grounded, tune into source, and focus on my breath. As you practice meditation daily, it will become easier and easier to stay focused and ultimately get to the point where you feel this outer body experience and Zen. Most people think that meditation is about emptying your mind from all thoughts. In reality, meditation is observing and listening. You allow your thoughts to come and go freely. You notice the thought then gently let it pass. Meditation allows you to tap into your heart coherence as well, which results in that higher vibration I discussed earlier. When you become a higher vibrational match for something, you create abundance.

That abundance flows freely. Abundance is always present, but you can create blockages against abundance. The most common way we create our own blocks is through fear. When you are fearful, you oftentimes have a lack mindset, meaning that resources are limited or you fear scarcity in some way, shape, or form. Or perhaps you think you aren't enough. That lack-minded perspective and fearful thoughts cancel out any positive intention. Fear is disguised as something that holds you back. Fear is limiting if you let it be. Fear keeps you stagnant and afraid to take that leap of faith forward. Rather than using fear to impede your abundance from flowing freely, use fear as something to propel you forward into abundance.

The next time you meditate, try a visualization meditation. Imagine you are opening a door with your keys. As you are unlocking the door, visualize that you are also unlocking opportunities that bring you closer to your heart's desires. You can also physically do this in everyday life. When you return home from running errands, unlock your abundance when you unlock your front door.

Meditation creates space to listen to what God, source, universe, or the Most High have to tell you. You sit back and let God speak to you because meditation frees up parts of your mind and creates space in your soul to receive.

Prayer

Prayer and meditation go hand-in-hand. I make it a priority to meditate and pray every single day. Ideally, I meditate and pray for fifteen minutes in the morning and again in the evening. Realistically, I carve out time for a quick couple-minute meditation and prayer in the morning before I start my day and a longer fifteen-minute chunk for meditation followed by prayer in the evening before I go to bed. Prayer is where you speak to God and claim your abundance and blessings. I always make it a point to give thanks and praises to the Most High during prayer. This is also the perfect opportunity to show gratitude for everything in your life.

Meditation and prayer together are so powerful, and they create magic. When you meditate, you are creating space for the blessings and abundance to flow effortlessly. When you pray, you claim those blessings and manifest the abundance you just created space for in meditation.

Manifesting is simple. Decide what you want. Since you are already a vibrational match for your desire once you are heart coherent, truly believe you can have it. Know you deserve it. Trust you are worthy of it. Believe it is yours. Act as though it is yours. Then watch it all come into fruition.

Every day, close your eyes and visualize for a few minutes having what you want, experiencing the feelings of already having or doing it. Say a prayer as if you already have manifested it. Then come back to where you are now. Focus on what you are grateful for already and what you enjoy right now. Go into your day and release those thoughts into the universe. Trust that the universe, God, or the Most High has your back. Manifestation happens when you start to emit your own frequency rather than absorb the frequencies around you, when you start imprinting your intent on the universe rather than receiving an imprint from existence. Manifestation starts with prayer.

Release

In order to move forward, you must release yourself from everything that weighs you down. Not everything that weighs you down is yours to carry. So ask yourself, "Is this really mine to carry? Does this support the life I am creating?" You also must release yourself from the stigma that a homemaker isn't enough. I know I struggled with this before we had children. It was so odd to me that my new role was to take care of the house and serve Maurice. I felt worthless on most days, just a waste of space. Hey, I am here breathing and following my fiancé/husband/lifelong partner around for his career.

I kept thinking that what I was doing wasn't enough. I thought once I had children this feeling would go away. I had new purpose in addition to the wife role and that was to be a mother. I was bringing life into this world and raising beautiful human beings. I was sadly mistaken. I still felt empty and believed that a homemaker and mother was not enough. I felt like I should be doing more. I should have been doing more—doing more of what drives me, doing more of what I am passionate about, and doing more to live in my purpose. Basically, doing more for myself.

But I am here to remind you that you don't find your worth in your husband, your children, or how clean and tidy you can keep a house. You find your worth within your own self. You need to take care of yourself. You will never find happiness until you let go of the illusion that your needs are less important than your husband's and kids' needs or that you need someone else to be complete. You are already a whole human. You are enough.

Reclaim

Shifting your mindset, becoming heart coherent, engaging in daily meditation, and praying will redesign your DNA, free ancestral trauma, allow you to master soul lessons that keep recurring, and cultivate space for the abundance flow that you are. Once you shift, you will realize you are not the same person you used to be. That is the point. You are not the same you. We just mourned and said goodbye to the old you. This shift and release welcomes the new you and allows you to reclaim yourself. You are taking back your identity and ascending it.

As that caregiver archetype shines dominantly through, you have to remember not to lose yourself in serving others. Not to worry if you have already lost yourself. It's never too late to reclaim yourself at any point in time. The beautiful thing is you get to reclaim yourself whenever you want and look, be, and feel like however you want to look, be, and feel. One way I reclaimed myself was by regaining my independence and redefining what independence meant to me, even though I was relying solely on my husband's income.

In this reclaiming process, you need to know that you can rise up from anything. After working this model, you will have established your humanhood again—a hood that is totally separate from motherhood and wifehood. You are allowed to completely reclaim yourself. Nothing is set in stone. You are not stuck. You have choices. You can think new thoughts. You can grow. You can learn new things. You can create new habits and routines. The only thing that matters is that you decide to rediscover yourself today and continue to journey forward. Love yourself with so much conviction and so much heart that it's nearly impossible to doubt just how capable you are, capable of becoming exactly who you have always wanted to be.

Heal Generational Trauma

Despite the rough patches and constant internal battles, you never lose value. I was emotionally run down, had to challenge my entire upbringing and cultural conditioning, and experienced the ridicule from family and friends. They told me I was wasting my life away by sitting around on my three college degrees. Just because I took countless jabs didn't mean I had lost value or I should think any less of myself.

You are still amazing regardless of what you have been through. You are wonderfully made. Despite how you feel now, you still have power. You have value to add into this world. Repeat after me, "I have so much value to add to this world."

But these beliefs come from generational traumas, oppression, and societal conditioning. Ever since the moment we were born, it has been embedded within us that we are supposed to work hard, long hours, meet someone, get married, take off for two to six weeks—just long enough to have the baby and physically heal from the birth (ignoring the psychological aspects altogether)—send the baby to daycare, return to work, maybe have another baby in a few more years, continue working until you're at least sixty-five, and then retire if you're lucky. Especially now, with gender equality, (let me make this clear . . . I am an advocate for equal pay for men and women) women get to have it all—a career, be a wife, raise our families, and take care of the household. Yes, have it all. That is dope. But is it possible to juggle it all?

With that said, I believe there is a subtle beauty in wanting to be at home, raise your family, and serve your husband, especially if you are in a position financially where you don't have to work. Or in some cases, you also work but your salary hardly covers childcare costs, so you think, "Why not stay at home?" Why not be involved with the shaping and guiding of your children? There is absolutely nothing wrong with wanting to stay at home and be a homemaker. Homemaking, for the record, is a challenging role. It is a respectable and admirable thing to do and totally underrated as one of the hardest roles in the world. You, as a homemaker, show up one hundred percent and in all of the hats you wear. If you feel compelled to take on this role, embrace it. Because while difficult, it is the most fulfilling and rewarding thing you'll ever do.

Please do not fall into the trap of negative self-talk or allow others to talk negatively about your choice to be home. I couldn't stand it when people asked me, "What do you do all day? Play with Juniper?" or "I mean, why can't you make this trip out here; it's not like you're working..." or "What, you just sit around all day? Must be nice!" or "It's real hard trying to keep yourself 'busy' huh?" Don't give those messages any power. If you do, that trigger of inadequacy can creep in. Release the stigma of choosing to be a homemaking mom and wife and redefine what it means to you. Release that insecurity. Negate the feelings that what you are doing is not enough. Because I am positive it is.

I am here to tell you that you are capable and you are enough. Being a homemaker is enough. Today I want you to think about all that you are instead of all that you are not.

Here's why it's enough. You are blessed to be able to stay at home and raise your family. You know how many working moms wish they had the opportunity to do what you're doing? More than you know. You get the opportunity to witness all aspects of watching your little humans grow with the freedom to go anywhere and do anything. This is that positive outlook that can shift and elevate your perspective about being a homemaker. You are able to play an active role in your children's lives.

For an even deeper fulfillment in your purpose ask yourself this: What reasons do you think your child's soul chose to use you as his or her portal to cross over to Earth side?" BOOM! Still think that staying at home to raise them isn't enough?

I know it's hard, mama. I know it can be hard to get up every day and have these little humans rely on you every minute. I know it's hard to feel like sometimes your world is so small. I want to remind you that you are their entire world. You are their nurturer, their home, their comfort. You are everything to them, and I hope, even on your hard days, you know how special you are, especially to your babes and husband.

It's actually pretty dope if you think about it. Someone asks you what you do, and you get to say, "I create and guide humans as they grow, and they teach me priceless information about myself and my higher consciousness for a living."

Has a light bulb gone off yet? If so, that is the conscious shift from a place of lack to a place of abundance. There's that positive perspective where you choose the truer statement.

If you truly feel called to pick up a hobby, have a side hustle, create an at-home business, go back to work full- or part-time, do it! You can be a fabulous mother and still follow your dreams. You, one hundred percent, can if you so desire, and it's something that has you walking in your purpose. But don't do it just because you feel obligated to or because you need something to say when someone asks you, "So what do you do now?" Don't go back to work because you feel like you should be doing more. I will say it again: Being a homemaking mom and wife is enough. You are enough.

Bottom line is you hold it all down. You are the ultimate lover and nurturer. You bring stability into your man's life. You enhance his life. You don't create problems because you create solutions. In fact, you are the solution. You shine light into his darkness. You inspire growth. You are that resilient woman. You may be hidden or buried underneath all of the fear, insecurities, societal norms and expectations, and cultural conditioning. But nonetheless, reclaim the woman you are because you are resilient, beautiful, powerful capable, and enough.

CHAPTER 8:

Embrace Self-Care

Step 5: Mother Yourself

Earlier in Chapter 4, I touched on the caregiver archetype. Although the caregiver is extremely compassionate and generous with giving themselves to others, often times, she finds it hard to create balance between being a caregiver to others and being a caregiver to herself. The main characteristic of the caregiver archetype is her desire to serve others and forget herself in doing so. She may come to resent the people she helps because she tends to burn out and deplete her energy. This is why it is so important to mother yourself the way you mother your children.

You must prioritize taking care of yourself so that your ability to maintain caregiving doesn't erode.

In a nutshell, you must learn to love yourself unconditionally, just as you love your husband and children.

Sounds easy, right? You're probably thinking I actually do love myself unconditionally. But how many times do you find yourself feeding your children before you feed yourself? How often do you realize you haven't eaten anything all day? How many times have you had to ask yourself if you actually brushed your teeth today? Have you even smiled today? How long has your hair been in that protective style without oiling your scalp? How long has your hair been up in that messy bun, untouched? When is the last time you even took a comb or brush to your hair? When's the last time you washed your hair? Do you take a quick birdbath more often than you used to? When's the last time you actually showered? You forgot to lotion or use body butter, huh? Did you get dressed today? Have you given yourself a compliment today? How about in the past week? Have you acknowledged what an amazing job you are doing at juggling all of your hats and roles? Do you carve out time for yourself? Have you worked out or made movement a priority? Have you done something you love doing in the past few days? Do you continually beat yourself down with negative self-talk? Are you wearing the same clothes from five years ago while your children and husband are sporting new outfits on the reg?

Yeah, you aren't loving yourself for real, sis. I need you to get on that immediately.

You have to love all up on yourself! Why? Because no one loves you the way you love you. I admire that no one can love Maurice more than Maurice. He will always take the time for himself and nothing or no one, not even me, can interfere with that. This mentality is what used to trigger me into resentment, but it's also one of the qualities I love so much about him. Remember, your partner is a mirror, and I am so glad that Maurice has exemplified what it looks like to really love yourself. His self-love only triggered me because it was an area I lacked and needed to draw more attention toward.

One of my favorite mantras, which I repeat in the mirror, is "I release my desire for others to be there for me when I have to be there for myself." Sounds like a no brainer to just show up for yourself, right? Wrong. We are programmed to believe that others have to meet our needs, when really we need to meet our own needs. We are so engrained to put ourselves last on the totem pole as mothers and wives that we forget we have to meet our own needs before we can meet anyone else's needs. You've likely heard the oxygen mask on a plane analogy before: Secure your own mask before assisting others. I used to laugh and say I would for sure put the mask over my child's face before mine. But how can you muster up the energy to put someone else's mask on when you are on your last breath? You have to mother yourself and place your mask on first.

It's not selfish to put yourself first. Certain selfishness is actually necessary. But in reality, being selfish doesn't have to be negative either. I am redefining what selfish means. It's not a bad thing to be selfish anymore. When you are selfish you are concerned with your own personal benefit, but how you use that personal gain is the key. You can't pour from an empty cup, but you cannot fill your own cup up unless you are somewhat selfish. You cannot serve others to the best of your ability unless you are self-serving. You cannot show up for your family when you aren't loving yourself, caring for yourself, and doing things that bring joy. How can you really be of the best service to them when you are haggard, run down, exhausted, and overwhelmed? You have to put yourself first. How can you show up for them if you can't even show up for yourself? How do you serve them if you aren't your best self?

Self-care is how I am able to support my husband through the hard times, the ugly games they should have won, or the rough days at practice. By mothering myself, I am able to care for Juniper with compassion, grace, and patience. Through loving myself I am able to have a comfortable, healthy, and thriving pregnancy.

You become your highest self when you are heart coherent, loving yourself, pouring into yourself, and doing things that bring you joy. It is then—once you are a whole person and filled up—that you can fulfill your duties as a wife and mother to the highest service. In addition, if you have others pouring into you as well, this creates overflow and abundance. You can re-commit to yourself as many times as you need to. The important part is that you continue to make a conscious decision and effort to show up for yourself, commit to yourself, and love yourself. Mothering yourself is how you take your power back.

Mothering yourself is on of the most difficult things for my clients to do. Speak love to yourself and watch yourself grow. Make it a daily effort to say one thing in the mirror that is loving.

"I am beautiful."

"I am so impressed with the meal I just made."

"I am taking care of business like a boss."

"I love my body."

"I love myself because I'm me."

"These tiger stripes of mine tell my beautiful story."

"I am doing the best I can."

"I am killin' it."

"I am a strong woman."

"I am enough."

"I am worthy of all things that serve me."

"I am worthy of love."

Here's another exercise to try: Make a list of the things that bring you joy. This is one of my favorite writing exercises, which I do with my coaching clients. You can write your hobbies, objects, activities . . .anything you want. It's an exercise with unlimited possibilities. It can be something simple as sitting in peace without being touched, or it can be something more active like hiking. This can be a running list that you post on your fridge or somewhere visible, and when you find something else that brings light into your life, add it to the list. This list should be easily accessible for whenever you are feeling down or need to refill your cup. It's easy to reference this list on the bulletin board in the kitchen and then do something on it. Self-care is doing the things that bring you joy (and not just manis and massages). Self-care is also a form of self-love.

Self-care doesn't always have to mean candlelit bubble baths, massages, facials, and all the pampering that comes to mind. It can be something as simple as setting boundaries. I had a client who is engaged to a professional basketball player, and I asked her to tell me about a time she recently said "no." She was immediately stumped, her face blank. She couldn't think of anything recent, so she told me about a time she said no a few months back. She has very relaxed boundaries and is always willing to do anything for everybody, which is amazing—don't get me wrong—but it's not okay when it starts to take a toll on your physical and spiritual body and wellbeing. She was not honoring herself; therefore, she was not loving herself or practicing self-care. Boundary-less people cannot protect their vibration. She was allowing anything and everyone to creep into her sacred space. Your aura should be impenetrable, and it was brought to my attention that she needed to set firm boundaries for others in order to love herself.

I asked a follow-up question: "How did you feel after you said no?"

She said she actually felt all right afterward. I loved this part! I reassured her that it is okay to say no and feel no remorse or guilt.

The power of *no* is huge. Whenever you say no, I encourage you to say it unapologetically and with no remorse. This can be applied to play dates, events, outings, favors—anything really. If you are not energetically aligned to do something, don't force it. Just say no and keep it moving. No explanation owed. The worst thing you can do is ignore that energetic dissonance, suffocate your feelings, lower your vibrations, and tuck your emotions in a box. The worst thing you can do is walk away from yourself when you are the thing that you need the most.

Your children don't need a perfect mom. They need a happy one. Likewise, your husband doesn't need a perfect wife; he needs a happy one. No one wants to be around a grumpy, uptight, miserable, stressed, and unpleasant person. The boundaries you create are put in place for a reason.

Anytime you feel good, you've found vibrational alignment with who you really are. Being in alignment is another way of showing up for yourself. Showing up for yourself is a simple way to mother yourself. In order to find peace, you have to be in alignment within. To truly enjoy life, you have to enjoy who you are. To enjoy who you are, you have to love yourself unconditionally. Once you understand this, you will be protected from everything that made you feel otherwise. With this newly found realization, you recognize yourself, even when you are alone, and you will never be lonely.

Meditation and pranayama (breath work) is also a form of mothering yourself. I touched on this earlier, but to refresh, when you pray, you speak to God, and when you meditate, God speaks to you. I love to meditate or just breathe with my eyes closed. Breathing goes hand-in-hand with moving energy, whether you are healing, manifesting, grounding, or slowing down. Conscious breathing has so many physiological and etheric benefits. Conscious breathing focuses your attention, sends prana, or life, into your body, ignites your internal fire/serpent power that is housed at the base of your spine, opens your chakras, and expands your state of consciousness. If you're not into the spirituality of breathing and need more science, conscious breathing lowers your blood pressure and oxygenates your brain and all of your cells. Either way you look at it, we are energetic beings and breathing turns the switch on.

Start off just as with any meditation. With your eyes closed, rub the palms of your hands together and place them on your heart. Breathe into your heart, sending prana, life force, into your palms. Imagine that energy and breath circulating the entire body starting from the heart and back out of the palms. Breathe into your palms and send new life into your heart, reversing that energetic flow. You will instantly love, feel love, and be loved.

You are a heroine, a divine feminine spirit, a queen, an oracle, a woman. You are someone to be admired and appreciated. Be the person who admires, appreciates, and loves you the most. Never be ashamed of how much you love yourself or how often you show yourself that love. Love fully, love completely, but most importantly, love unconditionally . . . and never apologize for it. Don't ever be sorry for loving yourself and mothering yourself.

CHAPTER 9:

View Situations from His Perspective

Step 6: See it Through Your Husband's Perspective

I know my husband sees this all differently. If I look at our situation from his point of view, I know that I will be more compassionate toward him and myself. Similarly, allowing your husband to see your point of view will allow you both to be on the same page. I know that I have to look at this objectively, the ability to differentiate between the story, which is what my psyche made up in my head to seem true, and the actual truth, or the facts.

As a professional basketball player, Maurice gets paid to perform. Every single day he goes to work, regardless of how he is feeling or how tired he is. He still shows up ready to work for himself, for us, and for his teammates. Basketball is a very physical sport, and he pounds on his body day in and day out. Even if he is sore, has aches and pains, or suffers with injuries, he still plays through. He sacrifices his body, physically and mentally exerting himself every single day so that I can be at home and raise our daughter and keep the house in order. Although his life hasn't appeared to have outwardly changed as dramatically as mine, the financial burden he is carrying has multiplied and continues to multiply as long as we multiply.

His "glamorous" and glorified job also comes with a lack of job security, instability, and a stressful, high-pressure, performance-driven work environment. This makes planning trips, vacations, and, well, life feel impossible, constantly waiting for the right time to set plans. And even when you set plans, things come up and change in an instant. Most of the time, teams can find a way to get out of their contractual obligations and cut you from the roster. Not to mention, there is a constant risk for injury that could set him back a few weeks, months, or worse, a season. Maurice has battled injury, and that's another mental and emotional aspect of his job that he has to deal with. Afterward, he was ready to step foot on the court mentally, but physically, he wasn't fully ready. As his partner, you are the one who has to stay strong, encourage your husband, lift him up, and hold it all together for him and for yourself too.

The team can release you or trade you through technical terms in the contract for underperforming, front office politics, or for whatever reason they see fit. He has to score baskets and win games because that's essentially what they pay him to do. Talk about competitive. I remember when we found out we were pregnant with Juniper, and then the Knicks waived his option for the upcoming season. He was jobless for nearly seven months. I could only imagine the stress and pressure weighing on him. And yet, he still continued to work out every single day (sometimes two and three times a day) and kept his unwavering faith throughout that uncertain time.

Yes, he is traveling and staying in hotels, ordering room service, and meanwhile I am dealing with a temperamental toddler who is also trying to navigate through big feelings that arise because sometimes daddy isn't always around. I am consumed with responsibilities and with managing everything at home, but I know he would love to be with us, bonding with Juniper and experiencing pregnancy with me. It took me a while to realize that he was missing all of these milestones and missing important memories that only Juniper, our baby in my womb, and I are sharing. It is devastating at times, and I feel bad that he doesn't get to share these moments with us. He gets left out a lot because he is gone all the time. Yes, he FaceTimes us whenever he can, and I try to take tons of pictures and record everything to send to him to include him, but it's not the same as being physically present. For some husbands, those pictures are the worst. They bring out sadness and expose the reality that he is unable to be as involved as he'd hoped he could be. Why would he want to see that if he can't be with us? If you are unsure, just ask your husband, and from there create a photo sharing album . . . or don't.

Sometimes I can't wait for Maurice to get back home so I can get some relief from the day-to-day duties. But I also realize that when he comes home, he needs a break too. When he does return from a road game, he is recovering from the long trip. He comes back drained. Also, that travel day back home is usually considered his "off day." Ha! Traveling is exhausting in itself, and then to call that your day off and have to wake up the next day and go to work for two-a-day practices, treatment before and after both practices, film, lifting, and stretching—it's all insane. Most of his off-day he spends sleeping. Totally understandable after a twelve-hour trip to Spain, a game and then another twelve-hour trip from Spain back to Russia, for example.

When you want to take a day off, think about how he never gets to take a day off. He's got responsibilities and obligations to you and the kids, just as you have to him, the kids, and yourself. Sure, he gets one day off a week at best, and on that day off I bet you he still has to go into the gym. Let's say he doesn't have to go to his job for treatment or "optional" shooting, he is spending his off day with the family, and as you know it, kids are draining. So, is it really an off day?

Similarly, your husband needs to unwind and unload after a long day, as do you. It's so vital that Maurice winds down after his long day at the gym. He normally gets home late evening or stays up late and sleeps in. I never understood this until I had kids. You know that constant battle between going to bed early or staying up and enjoying your alone time after you put the babes down for bed? Yeah, your husband deals with that same battle, too. Should he go to bed because he is tired, or should he stay up for a few more hours to unwind and enjoy solitude? What would you pick? I bet you generally choose to stay up and enjoy your peace and quiet, so just take that into consideration.

Another note, Maurice can't sleep after games. He stays up because he is so exhausted, yet wired, I guess. I can't quite describe it, but my client's husbands feel the same way—as I did, too, when I played. The adrenalin doesn't just disappear.

Maurice is also a late-night gym rat. Real hoopers understand how therapeutic a late-night gym session is. When he's alone and we are stateside, he goes in late and stays for hours shooting. When we were in Russia with him, he didn't work out late out of consideration for us. How sweet, right? He doesn't want to be out all hours of the night, taking away from our husband-wife time. But at the same time, he is sacrificing his potential for me. It's flattering and it's great that he thinks about us before leaving late at night to go shoot. But also, it makes me feel bad because I am the reason why he's not putting in extra work to hone his craft. I inhibited him from getting better. He is compromising his work ethic and limiting himself by skipping his late-night shooting sessions. The day we left Russia, he was back on his grind going to the gym late like he used to do, and I couldn't have been happier.

The worst time is around that mid-season slump, in December or January, or when you are so close to visiting him or him coming home. I know I pull the "I don't feel close to you nonsense" out of nowhere. When really there is just nothing to talk about. I know what he's doing, and he knows what I am doing because, by this time, we know each other's schedules, and we do the same thing just about every day.

Honestly, there is nothing new going on between the both of us, and the conversation gets stale. There is lots of silence. You feel energetic distance between you two grow, conversations get progressively worse, you have less and less to talk about, and you both become short in your questions and answers. Basically, it's a blah convo. There is no need to make this a thing, create issues, and pick fights. Just be understanding and let the blah convo run its course. It's not going to last forever.

The worst is when you have a great day, and then when it comes time to talk to your husband about it, you forgot because it happened a day ago because of the time difference. I encourage you to write down things you want to tell him about. Also, if you are up for it, ask him some open-ended questions, play either/or (give him two options). Use this time to get to know your spouse better on a more intellectual level, asking about aspirations and dreams or how he wants to leave his legacy. Ask him how he wants to contribute to the world, show him the most recent pictures and videos of the kids, or just leave him alone. I strongly suggest that you don't unload on him with your entire day all at once. Chances are he doesn't have the capacity to actually listen to an hour debrief at the end of his long day. If possible, spread those conversations out throughout the day or just pick a few big details to share with him.

It's an around-the-clock job. He doesn't get to clock in and out. His job never stops. He has to stay hydrated, eat well to fuel his body, lift, get extra shots up, practice, get treatment, study film, review scouting reports, work out, recover at home, attend appearance events, and so on. So when he comes home, he needs time to himself, away from work but also away from us. I have learned to give him that space. As soon as he walks in the door, I stop whatever I am doing and greet him with a big hug and kiss. I feel like it's the least I can do after he comes home. It shows my gratitude for him and all the sacrifices he makes for our family. I then leave him alone.

Would you honestly want to do what your husband does every day? Would you rather work one, sometimes two jobs, or go to school, and hardly get to see your family? That's a hard no for me. I pull from my experiences playing basketball professionally to see things through my husband's point of view, but you can do the same by putting yourself in your husband's shoes. Just imagine how you would feel if you worked your husband's job. How would you feel if you got in a rut on the court and you just couldn't perform the way you knew you were capable of performing? How would you react at home after your coach chewed into you at practice? How would you want your wife to act in those situations? Would you prefer her to run around bitter and hostile or considerate and understanding?

Does your husband like to talk about what happened at work or does he not like to bring the office talk home? Maurice doesn't like to mix the two, and that's okay. We will talk about games very briefly, and we don't talk about basketball extensively. His entire life is basketball. I am his escape from basketball so naturally, it makes sense that he doesn't want to talk to me about games, strategies, plays, or rotation. I have learned that after a bad game or day to just leave him alone. He deals with and processes things really well on his own. If it's really bothering him, he will bring it up. Figure out what suites your relationship best and rock with that.

There is also this delicate balance between sharing your own struggles and concerns with him and actually dumping all of your issues onto him. You want to be considerate because he needs to focus for practices and games, but you need to share your emotions with him because he is supposed to be your best friend and life partner.

For example, I wanted to talk to Maurice about how I was physically in pain and exhausted from this pregnancy. At the same time, he had just traveled thirteen hours, played thirty minutes total in the game, had a sore body and all, and traveled thirteen hours back to Russia. It's just not cool to dump it all on him. I opted to first recognize how he felt, and then proceeded to express how I felt, and decided to go to bed early shortly after the conversation. By doing this, it allowed me to empathize with him instead of disregarding his feelings altogether, express my feelings, and then action a solution. Sometimes as women, we just want to be seen and are not necessarily looking for a solution all of the time. We just want to be heard. So if that's what you need tell him.

Similarly, it's difficult to find the right time to talk about serious issues between his busy schedule, travel, and games. You have to time these important conversations around games, for example. We don't normally talk before games if I am stateside. I'll send him a video of Juniper wishing him good luck, and I might shoot a text along with that saying, "You're unstoppable. Have fun. I love you Honey Buns." If we are together, we keep the conversation light and to a minimum. After the game, I assess the vibe, and if he's not in a mood, we can have important conversations at or after dinner—once he has that time to unwind.

Aside from his job, he does help out around the house and with Juniper. He is doing what he knows how to do to the best of his ability. He has been totally compliant and totally on board with my crazy cloth diapering. He spends time with Juniper so I can quickly run to the grocery store (those trips are never quick with her) and get my other errands done. I am able to "pamper myself a little"—sleep, massage, wax, mani/pedi, bath, solitude, a hot lunch date with myself, or link up with friends. He takes some early morning shifts. He is the best dishwasher in the world. He even grabs groceries if I don't have time or forget an onion (he picks the sweetest fruit! And I always forget onions). Most importantly, he loves and encourages me. There are so many other little things he does, but it feels silly to list them all out. We aren't keeping tabs on what we do and how we contribute. What is really important is that you create an equal partnership, although it may appear unequal on the surface.

Honestly, I couldn't and frankly don't want to be in Maurice's position. I would never want to have to be in that high-stress, performance-driven, two-a-day, body aching all the time, nagging little injuries keep coming back, work environment ever again. And on top of that, have the added pressure to provide for my family. I have nothing but respect, gratitude, and love for my husband and what he does for our family day in and day out. Show your husband you love him and appreciate all he does by lifting him up more.

I asked my husband to weigh in on this topic and drop some insight to gain a better understanding:

"Professional athletes, in general, deal with a lot of stress, both mentally and physically. Then you have the emotional aspect that comes with the job, too—bad performance, battling injuries, and even dealing with playing time. So, taking care of business at work and then coming home to spend quality time with my family and doing little things to give my wife some alone time and help lessen her load is not easy at all. But if you compare our lives with our wives' lives, they not only have to care for us and all of the things that come with us (stress, emotions, moodiness, exhaustion, absence), but also care for the kids and themselves.

I think spending time with Juniper as often as I can so my wife can rest or have time for herself helps tremendously. Waking up early to get her is helpful, too. You also gotta understand that our wives are so hands-on that it's hard to find ways to get involved. I guess you can say they also have their own routine and ways of doing things.

In the offseason, I am able to spend more time with my family but still struggle to help out on little things. I wish I could make her a good breakfast or just make something healthy to eat on a consistent basis. What most people don't realize is that the offseason is the only time I have to take care of things going on in my life—rehab and recover if needed, workout, visit friends and extended family, vacation, and all of the other things I had put off for the past eight to ten months. What is supposed to be summer for most people is the time for pro athletes to jam everything they have to do into a span of two to three months.

The women in our lives are the real heroes here. They are being pulled in different directions, and yet, they still get the job done. If anyone is strong enough to take on all of this, it's my wife, and she shows love and compassion while doing it. All I can do is be there for her, let her know I hear her, tell her I see her, and try to understand how she feels."

Ugh, don't you just love him? I sure do. I will touch on some of the other points he made in later chapters, but I wanted to leave you with this: try understanding your husband more. His life isn't as easy as you think, and your life isn't easy either. By better understanding each other, you can work together to find what works. I am all for creating an equal partnership, but sometimes you will carry more of the load and other times, he will. It fluctuates depending on the circumstances. That doesn't mean it's unequal.

Chapter 10:

Balance His Cameos and Your Routine

Step 7: Find Your Normalcy

It is a constant battle to balance your routine when he's around and when he's gone. It's very hard to get adjusted, and when you finally do get into the swing of things, he shows up and throws it all off. It can be frustrating. Especially during seasons such as when you just got a solid nap schedule down, are in the process of dropping a nap, just conquered nighttime sleep, or the kids are finally used to him being gone. It can feel like your entire world crumbles when he comes back home. (Yes, you are also rejoicing because he's back, and you missed him.) Whether his cameo is just for a few days or for the entire offseason, it's always an adjustment. There is this balance of creating a life with him while he's home rather than when he comes home, fitting into your life. He can't feel good knowing that when he comes home, he messes everything up. So you must find ways to incorporate your essentially separate lives and integrate them into one regardless of the duration of his visit.

Routine

My daily routine is not really a routine. I like to call it a loose pencil outline. I generally follow the same daily structure but leave tons of room for whatever arises that day (coaching clients, teaching yoga, local events, play dates, shopping, doctor's appointments, and life's surprises). With my loose outline of things I intend to get done that day, I also like to block my day in three-hour chunks. Within each block, I list a few to-dos. The to-dos are not set for a specific time but ideally the tasks get accomplished during that block of time. Of course, I have appointments and certain things that need to happen at a specific time, so this way of scheduling gives me a balance of flexibility and rigidness.

Here is a sample schedule:

6:00 a.m.-9:00 a.m.

- Meditation/Prayer
- Shower/Get dressed
- Feeding/Breakfast
- Get Juni dressed
- Unload and load dishwasher
- Activity/Independent play

9:00 a.m.-12:00 p.m.

- Teach yoga
- Lunch

12:00 p.m.-3:00 p.m.

- Juni naps (12:00–2:30)
- Coaching clients
- Personal/Spiritual development
- Tidy up

3:00 p.m.-6:00 p.m.

- Get dinner started
- Run errands
- Yoga/Sweat/Move

6:00 p.m.-9:00 p.m.

- Play/Cuddle
- Feed Juni
- Juni in bed (7:00)

- Eat dinner
- Clean up

9:00 p.m.-11:00 p.m.
- Plan for tomorrow
- Me time/Us time
- Bed

I generally start my day off the same regardless of whether or not Maurice is home. Juniper used to wake up at 6:00 a.m. on the dot every single day. Ugh! I used to dread waking up on most days because I was so drained from life. I cringed when I heard her whine at 6:00 a.m., and on top of that, it was still dark outside in Russia. Needless to say, I didn't used to start my days off on the best note. Also, I used to change how I started my day depending on if Maurice was home or not, and that was not working out for me. The inconsistency and unpredictability drove me nuts, and eventually I stopped my routine altogether and ended up lounging around the house all day in my pajamas (let's be real, I was probably naked), which made me even more unmotivated and unproductive, and that made me even more stressed and overwhelmed.

Now, Juni wakes up consistently around 6:15, and I make it a point to wake up before she does at 6:00 every day. If I am feeling ambitious, I'll set my alarm for 5:45. Just those fifteen to thirty extra minutes gives me time to myself—to meditate, get dressed and ready myself for the day ahead. It makes it so much easier to attack the day when you are ready for the day before the kids wake up. Otherwise, you are playing catch up all day long and realize the day has passed. Then you ask yourself what in the world you did all day. Yes, we all have those unproductive days, but that shouldn't be the norm. Eventually, my goal is to wake up one hour to thirty minutes before to work out, meditate, and get dressed. But you see, how this pregnancy is set up, it's getting harder and harder to move. Some days I don't even have the energy to peel myself out of bed, but somehow, I manage to find a way to get up. So for now, I will cherish the fifteen minutes of alone time I use to start my day off right.

Normally, I wear yoga pants. On a great day, I put on real clothes. My go-to outfits are dresses now. Pants and I have a hate-hate relationship, and dresses are the easiest way to look like you tried, but it's actually less clothes you have to wear and less you have to coordinate, unlike a whole entire outfit. On a blah day, this could be no clothes or a robe. I do my best to get dressed because, for some reason, clothes set the tone for the day. Even if I am tired, I will throw on a cute sunnie, and all is well with the world. Otherwise, the day drags, and it feels like I am automatically behind and drowning in tasks. Another thing to mention is that when you start your day at the same time as your kids, you find yourself showering at inopportune times, like during their naptime. That's cool if that works for you. There are times when that makes the most sense. But wouldn't you rather spend naptime doing something you love instead of getting ready for a day that's halfway over?

So my whole morning jam with feeding, diaper, and getting juniper dressed in the morning takes about thirty to forty-five minutes because it's filled with kisses, cuddles and a distracted nursing session. (Yes, I'm proud to still be breastfeeding at eighteen months.) This is our time to bond, and she babbles on about her dreams and whatever wisdom she is dropping on me. After I get her fed, we eat breakfast together. I'll make a giant smoothie for myself and Juniper jacks my straw even though I give her a different cup. Or if Maurice is in town, I'll plan for breakfast to be ready later when he wakes up. This past season, he had evening practice, so by the time he would get extra shots up or lift or and do treatment, he would get home between 9:00 and 10:00 p.m. But he is so wired up that he takes time after his dinner to unwind and relax. That means late nights for him, which lead to late mornings. Whereas for me, it's sometimes late nights to spend quality time with him and early mornings with Juniper. This all still happens even when I am sick, near death, flu-ridden, or a walking delirious zombie. This mom and wife thing stops for nothing.

I strongly suggest you take a second look at my sample block outline and then draft your own. I keep mine on the kitchen island. And whatever tasks I don't finish in that block, I try to move them to later in the day, push to the following day, or just forgo them totally. Either way, this method helps be become super intentional during the day and frees up my mental capacity by negating the thinking needed to determine what's to come next. It's already written down, so I can just glance at it and keep it moving.

I wish I could draft a sample pencil outline for the offseason, but the truth is there is no schedule or magical formula we follow to find our jam and rhythm. Everyday looks totally different, but that's what I love the most about it. It's not the same old, mundane routine. I will say that I rely heavily on my calendar whether Maurice is home or away. I am always adding future events, programs, lessons, trips, and appointments. I go to our city's events list online and add everything we are interested in on the calendar. You can also look at the park district magazine for classes and activities, too. Even if it's unlikely we will go to the farmer's market, then Storytime at the library, and then the Make a Mega Mess with Foam event at the children's museum all in the same week, I still put it on the calendar. I like to give myself the freedom and flexibility to choose what I feel like doing in that moment on that day. Maybe it is all three events or maybe it is none.

As the days close in, I'll look at the upcoming week and make a loose outline to ensure that we get the necessary things accomplished. From the loose week I outline, we take a few minutes to talk about the next day. Essentially, we plan the night before and map out our next day. This just allows us to get on the same page and get in rhythm so we both know what's going on. Also, there is no way I can remember every little thing. Calendaring is the best way to describe how I embrace Maurice's cameos. Routines, schedules, or outlines alleviate the pressure for me and takes the thought out of the day. I can just flow freely because the day is already laid out and unfolds effortlessly.

It's okay if the day doesn't go according to your plan. Leave some wiggle room for those precious moments of stillness and the crazy events that make you drop everything you intended to get done that day. We all know how news from a phone call can end up taking up your whole day. Or something random pops up unexpectedly and throws your day off. No need to stress or worry. It is all good. Everything that needs to get done will get done . . . eventually.

Plan Ahead

Now that we have a loose routine in place, it's best to plan for when he's around. A few days to a week before he comes home, start planning accordingly. Surrender your attachment to a specific outcome and instead focus on the resolution. If it's a quick little cameo, this may mean putting the babes down for an earlier nap, going to the store to buy extra groceries for the hungry man, clear the kids' and your schedules for the day. Maybe you let the kids stay up later or nap in daddy's arms instead of the crib since he just got back from a long road trip. Expect and embrace the organized chaos—or just plain chaos—when he's home. It's okay. It is easy to dwell on it and become overwhelmed because of the changes, but stay present. Surrender to what is.

If he's home for the offseason, you all will get adjusted after a couple weeks and find what works for everyone. You will make it work for your family. Whether he is home for a day or three months, make sure you include him in your life, don't just make him feel like he's messing up your jam (even if he is throwing it all off!). It may take some time for the kids to adjust to his physical presence, especially toddlers and younger kids. They could get super paranoid and sensitive whenever your husband leaves the house to go work out or run to the store now that they are of understanding age. Every time he walks out the door, they freak out because they think he's leaving the country again. Or they could be super clingy and never want to let you go. Either way, you all will get into your groove eventually, as long as you plan ahead.

Be Flexible

Be flexible, understanding, and adaptable. When he is home for the offseason, he has so many people and places to visit, and he still has to work out. This can make you feel like you are not his priority, but that's not true. He's gone out of the country or been in season for eight to ten months out of the year and has to cram everything and everyone into two to four months. Don't let this bother you. All you can do is be understanding and supportive. You cannot be upset with him because you feel entitled to more of his energy than he is able to give you access to. You must find that energy from within. Also, designate a date night. He's all yours for an hour a week. Maybe you can get ready for bed together. You can even make Sunday a family day. It's so important and worth it in the grand scheme of things.

The two to four months of the year when Maurice is off is what I look forward to most. Maurice gets more time off depending on where he plays (NBA or overseas), if the team makes the playoffs, how far they advance in the playoffs, and if he is playing on the Senegal national team. This past offseason was basically nonexistent. He came home from Russia in mid-June after making it to the finals and then had to report back to the same team mid-August. Imagine how many things piled up on our offseason to-do list. Now try and complete it all in two months while spending time with your wife, kids, friends, all while working out to stay in shape for the next season. Easy, right? All power moves are made in the offseason whether it's buying a house or a car, moving, or vacation. These things are done in addition to all of the little things he has to take care of.

We have a tax-deductible nonprofit foundation called the Maurice Ndour Foundation, so the summer is when we go to Senegal for our Basketball & Youth Empowerment Camp. Summers are insane for us, but we still manage to carve out time for ourselves and for each other. Though it seems impossible and as if it takes a ton of planning—and Maurice is not a planner, so it's like pulling teeth to sit down with him and plan out an offseason calendar—it's doable. He likes to just go with the flow, which I am all for, but I also want to make the most out of the time he has at home. I make sure he has a plan to get everything he needs to get done (partially for him and mostly for me because I will end up doing whatever he didn't get around to when he leaves again). We make it work by being flexible.

Smile

At the end of the day or when you feel that mid-day slump, take a minute to close your eyes and call all of the energy that you've exerted and given away back into yourself. We are energetic beings. This will recharge you. When all else fails, just smile, or laugh. Smiling for thirty seconds, even if you're not happy, makes your brain think you're happy and subsequently, you feel happy. Smile to show compassion for yourself too. This doesn't have to be as stressful and serious as you are making it. Just roll with the punches and go with the flow.

You don't have to be so hard on yourself. The beauty of it all is that you get to choose what your routine looks like. You are allowed to make whatever changes you need to and make adjustments as you feel are necessary. Regardless, you are doing what you feel is right and that's all that matters.

It's easier to live life once you accept the inevitable, accept what you can control. The chaos is yours to change. It doesn't stay the same. One day can be more hectic than others. Some days are filled with more energy than others. Some days are more frustrating than others. The difficult things vary. The challenges oftentimes pile on top of you, but the joy remains and grows. It won't be like this forever. Because in the end, you are resilient. You are adaptable. You rise.

CHAPTER 11

Gather Your Tribe

Step 8: Build Support

Surrender

As a mother, you are designed to be strong, independent, loving, resilient, resourceful, adaptable, and know how to find a way to make it all happen. That's the mama magic you possess. It's a beautiful thing. The flip side of that is when all of those bold, amazing qualities become crippling. When the strong, independent, loving, resilient, resourceful, adaptable mom turns into a reluctant, exhausted, overwhelmed, sad, bitter, and resentful being. That's generally what happens when we don't reach out for help.

As a mother we feel like we can do it all (which is one-hundred percent true). Here's the caveat: We do not have to do it all on our own. I was reluctant to ask for or even receive help. Why? Because I didn't want to inconvenience anyone, having them rearrange their busy schedules to accommodate me. I knew they had things going on in their lives, too, so I just didn't want to bother or burden them.

Recently, I had to go to urgent care because I had been sick for about a week, but the last three days, I had a fever, chills, aches, burning eyes, cough, and congestion—all that nasty flu-like stuff. I felt like death and couldn't function, which is odd because I can almost always function no matter how sick I am. I normally don't even get sick and when I do, it's mild and I bounce back quickly.

I was at home in Scottsdale, Maurice was in Russia, and my family lives in Chicago. I have a few good people in my circle I can always call, but I was so reluctant to call and ask for someone to watch Juniper while I went to urgent care. Maurice saw how much I was suffering and how terrible I looked on FaceTime, and he asked me why I didn't call Caliph, his basketball trainer. I huffed and puffed and rolled my burning eyes. I told him that I didn't want to. I would deal with it myself. We finished our convo and then minutes later Caliph called me basically yelling at me and asking me why I hadn't called him and told him I was really sick and needed medicine or to go to the doctor. He had his stern voice on because he was kind of angry about hearing about my illness from Maurice instead of from me. He said we were family and that whenever I needed *anything,* he would get it for me or have someone get it to me if he was unable to. He made Maurice that promise a long time ago, that he would look out for us and watch over us. He reassured me that he is here to take care of us, especially while Maurice is out of the country.

All during Caliph's rant, these words really stuck: "You can do almost anything on your own, but sometimes you need a little help." He kept repeating that in his stern, concerned voice. It was almost like he knew what I needed to hear. I was on the verge of tears at that point because I knew that I needed help all along, but I was just too stubborn to admit it. It felt good to know that someone genuinely wanted to care for me, and I wasn't a burden to him. It was a relief to have that "permission" to ask for help. Caliph didn't actually give me permission to ask for help. He just gave me the space to ask. He made it very clear that it was okay to need help, and he expected me to ask for help when I needed it. But did I ask for anything? Of course not.

The next morning, I felt worse. I continued my naturopathic and over-the-counter remedies but still no relief. I checked in with Maurice. He couldn't understand me. I was so miserable, and yet I still wouldn't utilize my resources. Why? Because I had this story going on in my head about why Caliph probably couldn't come.

"Caliph is the best basketball trainer, and this is the peak time for training and workouts with his clients. I don't want to inconvenience him as he's got a full day with clients and workouts already scheduled. There's no way he can step away from work to help me out and have to cancel his workouts."

I had to differentiate between the story, which is what my psyche felt was true, and the actual truth, the concrete facts. That mumbo jumbo was all story. The fabricated reasons why Caliph couldn't or wouldn't come help were all story. To find a truer statement, I had to ask, "When people ask me for help or when someone asks me to do something for them, how do I truly feel?"

I love extending a helping hand to anyone in need. I am almost always happy, willing, and able to accommodate anyone, especially if it promotes health and wellbeing. Helping people makes me feel good and rewarded. So, I had to look at this from that perspective and afford Caliph the opportunity to feel good for helping someone in need. Not to mention, he repeatedly told me to call when I needed help.

I finally surrendered and called Caliph the next afternoon. He was happy to hear from me. He said he was on his way so he could watch Juniper while I went to urgent care. Once I hung up the phone, I immediately felt the dis-ease leave my body. My symptoms alleviated and basically all physical discomfort subsided. The fear of being a burden, suffering in silence, and the whole made-up story of asking for help caused my body to become dis-eased. Crazy right?

But when I realized I was experiencing this for a specific reason, I leaned in and found the lesson to be learned. It was actually kind of annoyed that I felt this instant relief because at that point, I didn't really need to go to urgent care anymore (I still went though). I felt energetically recharged just by having this realization and surrendering to the feeling that I can't do everything on my own. Please know that you display so much power when you ask for help, contrary to popular belief.

The whole time I was letting my ego get in the way. Do not let your strength become your biggest weakness. Do not let your strength become self-destructive. Don't let pride or insecurities make you feel inadequate, weak, for less of a mama because you reach out for help. It is actually the opposite. Asking for help is a sign of strength, not weakness. You are very powerful, and it takes strength and courage to admit that you need help and then accept that help. You are capable. You are enough. You just need a little help from time to time.

Another big reason why I never used to ask for help is because if you ask my family, I have OCD (obsessive compulsive disorder). But I would say I am just particular about how things are done and where things go. Either way, if I asked for help, I knew the task wouldn't be done to my liking, or I would think I could have done it way faster and more efficiently myself. I also know my husband would agree with those aforementioned statements. He actually said so in Chapter 9. He said that women are very hands-on and heavily involved, so much that it becomes extremely difficult to help out.

You have your own routine and are used to doing things on your own all the time, but you have to let your husband get involved. Part of the responsibility lies on him to proactively help out and just do things, but on the other hand, he doesn't know how to help out or his efforts fall short when he does help out. It's essentially a loose-loose situation. But you have the power to show him what he can do, how to do it, and include him more. Loosen up the reigns a bit and be open to different ways of accomplishing the same task.

I remember my husband was loading the dishwasher and I know for a fact he felt my eyeballs on the back of his neck. I was just staring at him, watching him load the dishwasher incorrectly. I then made a comment about where to put a certain dish. Immediately I regretted saying anything. I thought to myself, "Just let him help! Let him do it the way he wants to do it. In the end, the dishes are out of the sink and it's one less thing you have to do." And if he loaded it up so that some dishes stuck together and didn't get all the way clean, so be it. So what if a couple of dishes have to get re-washed? It's still less work for me to do that than to have do all the dishes myself. He was trying his hardest to help me out and to show me that he cares. Let your husband help and be happy about it. Isn't that was you wanted after all?

My husband was saving me from doing one less task that evening and, for that, I appreciated all of his effort. It's perfectly fine to surrender to tasks not getting done the exact way you normally would do it. It's okay if things are not done to your standards. It's okay to be a little lax and hands-off when you accept help. When you ask for help, just know it will get done—probably not your way—but it will get done one way or another. And be grateful that you have someone ready and willing to assist you.

Once you ask for help, you have nothing to worry about. The burdens are lifted from your shoulders and are no longer only yours to carry. When you allow someone to help you with a heavy load, it's no longer heavy because the weight is distributed to the helper(s).

It's okay to ask for help. It's normal to ask for help. When you are open to receiving, help you also are open to receiving abundance. I love me some abundance! Abundance, in this case, can look like extra time, support, rest, ideas, energy, prosperity, or peace of mind.

How to Ask for Help

When asking your husband for help, make sure you do it the right way. Yes, there is a wrong way. There's nothing worse than coming home from a long rough day at the gym where coach chewed you out at practice to stand in front of a nagging, miserable wife. Ew, no thank you!

When he comes home, stop whatever you're doing, smile, and greet him at the door. *Do not ask him to do anything. I repeat. Do not ask him to do a thing right now.* This sets the tone for the evening (or day, depending on what time he comes home). You have just created a space for him to let go of whatever happened at the office and be embraced by a loving, supportive, and compassionate wife. Give him time to unwind and be alone for a little bit. After he's had time to himself in his own space, he should understand that it's only fair to be present and show up for you. Now, you can ask him how his day was, how he's doing, share something from your day, or talk about anything that you need from him.

There's a suggested way to ask him for help. I am not discouraging you from asking for help. I just have seen from experience that husbands are more willing to help and consistently do more tasks around the house when you reach out this way.

First, explicitly state what you need. How is he supposed to know that you need help unless you open your mouth and tell him? It may seem obvious to you that you are drowning in mounds of laundry, but he doesn't know that you want his help. If you don't ask for help you won't receive help. With that said, there will be no nagging, whining, complaining, or passive aggressiveness we women are notorious for. This is not the time to beat around the bush or drop hints because he won't notice or understand what you really need him to do anyways. He is no mind reader, and really isn't one to decipher what you say versus what you really mean. No time to play games.

One thing that I will probably never get over is when he leaves his plate on the table after a meal or puts a dirty dish in my perfectly clean, empty sink. It drives me nuts. Did you not just see me cook dinner and then watch me wash all of the dishes, dry them, and put them away, and you are really going to even think about setting something in that sink for me to wake up to in the morning? Instead of making a snippy comment, such as, "This dirty dish won't wash itself," or "these dirty dishes better be out of this sink when I wake up," or dropping hints about how long it took me to clean up after dinner, I just ask him to wash his dish before he comes to bed. It's that simple. I am direct and use a nice tone. Problem solved! He may not move immediately, but I know that when I wake up the dish will not be in the sink.

Next, ask him to do something or if he asks what he can do, make sure you are clear, concise, and use as few words as possible. That last part is critical—use as few words as possible. I used to go on and on about some task, and he would walk away to go do it and then come back seconds later and ask about a detail he missed. I elaborately told him every small detail he needed to know, which was too much unnecessary detail for his liking. Just get to the point and mention the need-to-knows. I swear men hear every fifth word or whatever, so be short with your request, but be as detailed as possible to ensure you get your point across, and he will actually do as he is asked.

Third, make it an expectation that he helps out. You can delegate reasonable tasks for him to complete when he is home. Trash is Maurice's go-to (although I do find myself taking the trash when he's not home, but it's okay), and he's been on the dishes a lot lately. Maurice has been the man on dishes. When my first trimester hit me hard with two- and three-day long migraines and bouts of nausea, he stepped up his game and was there to wash dishes just about every day for me. He also did so many other little things that really helped me out. You all just don't understand. I love my Honey Buns!!!

Finally, praise him once he's done the job. Sounds stupid right. Like why would you praise a grown man for taking out the trash when that's what he's supposed to do? Yes, he is supposed to help you because that's what you do in a partnership, but the praise isn't for that reason. The praise signifies your gratitude for him and his willingness to share the household responsibilities. (Yes, responsibilities are shared unequally, but it's all good because you have an equal partnership still.) Praise him regardless of how well he completed the task.

"Thanks for taking that heavy trash out."

"I appreciate you loading those dishes for me."

"Aw, you beat me to changing her diaper. You're the best"

"Thanks for wiping down the sticky kitchen countertops."

Even if he just pushed the crumbs off the countertop onto the floor, it doesn't matter. Say thank you anyways. There's nothing that can tear your man down faster than when you constantly go behind him to fix what he just did or his efforts go unnoticed and unappreciated. This is so discouraging and makes him not want to help. He might even stop helping all together because he doesn't see the point in trying to do anything because it's not done right, according to you. Regardless of if it's done to your standards, be appreciative, and give thanks to him because this will make him more inclined to want to continue helping. When you praise him for contributing, you make him feel needed. He will want to help out even more now that he knows you need him and rely on him.

After you ask for help in the way your husband is actually able to receive your request, you find this common ground of understanding. He understands where you are coming from and what you need from him. After some time, eventually your spouse will see what you need before you ask for it. That is what I live for. Asking the right way creates this mutual understanding, and that's what it is all about. Understanding each other harmoniously so that you can find what works for you both.

Another thing to take into consideration is to understand how your husband was raised and understand how he is wired. Your case may not be as culturally extreme as mine, but still it can apply. My husband is Senegalese, and in their culture, the fathers don't play a hands-on role in raising their children until they are a few years old. This was wild to me at first. I couldn't quite fathom this, but after I visited Senegal and saw the family dynamic, including more traditional gender roles, everything about Maurice began to make even more sense. The men love babies and their children. I was surprised to see how many Senegalese men took Juniper out of my arms and how happy they looked holding a baby. But when they were done, they were done. Handed her right back to me or to their wives. I say this to make the point that your husband is doing what he knows how to do to the best of his ability. Again, it's your responsibility to understand this and use that awareness to find that common ground.

From Maurice's standpoint, him going to work and expecting a meal on the table when he comes home isn't too much to ask for. It's the norm where he's from. In the beginning for me, it is asking for a lot. I do my best to do that for him, but it's not just realistic for me to do that every single day. I have accepted that. It doesn't make me any less of a woman or wife. It just means there is room for growth and an opportunity to ask for help. He feels loved when I do this one thing for him.

The other reason why there was always a hot meal on Maurice's table is because women in Senegal are not expected to do it alone. They are surrounded by a community of women who assist one another. The women cook all of the meals each day, take care of the children, and clean the house. Men will go to work and play with the babies for a little bit, but that baby is mostly taken care of by the mother, grandmother, and the women in their circle. They have other women in the kitchen cooking with them. They have a group of women supporting each other, uplifting each other by making up for where the others lack. A collective of women make it possible to carry out the various roles of women. Community is exactly what we are missing in millennial motherhood. We are expected to carry out all of our roles as if we have the same community structure as back in the day or as they do in other cultures.

That trip to Senegal was life-changing for me. I realized I was doing the work of a whole group of women. I was trying to be this perfect wife, clean, cook three delicious meals a day, and also be the best mother to Juniper all by myself. Like what? After returning from Senegal, I made it a point to build my support system.

Build Your Circle

Build a support system that is in alignment with you. When you are doing the things you enjoy and love, you will naturally gravitate toward other individuals with whom you click. When you connect with people who are good for you, you feel it. It's that energetic resonance that stems from being heart coherent, as mentioned in Chapter 7. This is a huge deal. Realize how great it is to be around someone who lights you up.

It's okay to admire someone else's beauty without questioning your own. You can admire someone else's choices and ways of doing things without doubting your own. It's powerful beyond belief when you ask for help. It's only right for you to receive help and function as a collective. Women uplifting women. Women empowering women. It's a beautiful thing to witness and an honor to be a part of.

Connection is why we are here, and it's how we are wired. Connection is what unites us all together. The ability to feel connected is what we need in order to thrive. It takes courage to tell the story of who you are with your whole heart. You have to let go of who you should be and just be yourself in order to make a real connection. It is courageous to be imperfect.

Embrace vulnerability. What makes you vulnerable makes you beautiful. This is what makes you . . . you. Vulnerability is absolutely necessary to create connection and community. Vulnerability, according to Brené Brown, is the core of shame, fear, and our struggle for worthiness, but it's also the birthplace for joy, creativity, belonging, and love.

One of my clients, who is married to an NBA player, told me that she battles daily with feelings of isolation and aloneness. Some days are better than others, of course. But she felt if she had more of a community, she wouldn't have as intensely hard days. I love helping women do exactly that—make them feel like they belong, show them that what they do matters, and create built-in support.

With the nature of my husband's job, we are constantly moving, seldom in the same place for long. This makes finding community unappealing and pointless. By the time we get settled and actually find our new tribe, it's time to leave again. So always shifting community is what seems to be the most challenging. You barely have time to grow roots before it's time to uproot again. It can be profoundly discouraging. Why even bother trying to establish your sense of community if you are going to leave soon anyways? The answer? When you are connected, you feel worthy and have a sense of belonging. Women who are worthy and feel a sense of belonging are also connected.

You have to still put yourself out there to find your community, regardless of the duration of your time in that home, city, or country. You have to plant yourself anyways and expect to grow roots. Even if you don't ever get a chance to really grow those roots deep before you leave that city, you are still connecting, and this makes you feel like you belong and that you are worthy. If you don't connect and build your sense of community, you will float through life feeling empty. If you don't actively seek out your community everywhere you go, you are limiting yourself and missing out on opportunities to connect with beautiful souls, even if it's just for months, days, or even an hour. You will never feel worthy or like you belong if you don't let your guard down and find your community. It doesn't matter if it's for a day or few years, you need your community to thrive. You need your community to feel supported. It's up to you to decide what community looks like to you.

Date

Sounds silly, but you have to basically date again. I know you already found your lifelong partner and thought the dreaded process of dating was over for good . . . but sorry. You're sadly mistaken. Dating is not over. In order to find your tribe, you have to put yourself out there again. It's easy to get so wrapped up in your daily routine that you never leave the house or make time to cultivate relationships. Nothing good ever stemmed from Mommy Jail and comfort zones but stagnancy and complacency. How can you build your support system if you don't get out and meet people? You have to make a conscious effort to leave the house at least once a day.

You'll feel better when you get out and you give yourself a chance to run into someone who shares in similar hobbies or values. I mentioned before that I look at our city website for events and activities. I also check out the local museums, libraries, and parks. Sounds like small talk and forced smiles, huh? The thought of listening to a group of women venting about how hard their lives are sounds like the absolute worst pity party. I get it. Superficial, meaningless conversation at the park gets old quick. It doesn't have to look that way though. When you naturally connect with someone it is on a deeper level.

I encourage you to research local community events, concerts, and Facebook groups. I promise there's a group for everything on Facebook. I'd like to think I am a cool mom, so Facebook is just not really it for me. Instagram is where it's at in my world. But in reality, Facebook has more opportunities for moms to connect and find interest-based groups in specific areas. Go to a meet-up. You'll be pleasantly surprised by the people you meet. I have met some pretty dope individuals from my local baby-wearing group and cloth diaper group, both of which I am extremely passionate about. I even became a baby-wearing educator (who knew that was even a thing?).

It's simple. Do the things you love, and you'll meet people you love. I've attended vegan festivals, vegan food fairs, farmer's markets, outdoor concerts, art walks, mommy and me yoga, open play for the kids, splash pads, park days, and so many other things. I have added these lovely ladies to my collective.

It will feel so weird, but I always encourage my clients to put themselves out there again. Get creative and think outside the box. Don't only look for kid-friendly activities but also things for yourself. Trust me, it is one hundred percent possible to get away for a guilt-free hour to enjoy doing something you love. I love suggesting finding a place to volunteer. Not only are you giving back to your community, but your community is giving back to you. It's a win-win. There are volunteer opportunities where toddlers and young kids are welcome to participate. Another place I encourage clients to look is at café flyers and bulletin boards. If you're anything like me, you can always find a hipster café with weekly events.

The bottom line is don't let being in a foreign city or the newness of motherhood (this includes naps and sleep learning) make you feel trapped and isolated. Do more of what you enjoy doing and you'll meet people you vibe with. It's as simple as that.

Hire Help

Another way to build this support system is to find a sitter. This topic gets a little sensitive with some mamas. Just because you need a sitter or a nanny doesn't make you less capable or a bad mom. You are enough. Hiring a sitter or a nanny, even for a couple of hours a few times a week, can be recharging for you. You don't have to feel guilty that you need a break and time for yourself. I understand that you are at home for a reason—for you to raise your kids, not some lady you hire. But you shouldn't feel guilty that you want to get away. In fact, you actually need to get away because everyone benefits from your little escape.

It's hard to find a good sitter or nanny, especially if you are new to the city, don't know many people around you, or don't speak the same language. So, my first recommendation is to use your family. They are there for a reason. Choose a family member who respects your parenting style and will not undermine or ridicule the choices you make. If that is not a viable option, (maybe you don't live near them or don't have that kind of relationship), find a sitter via word-of-mouth. I generally trust the sitter if someone recommends them to me from experience. Use those handy Facebook groups to ask for referrals. Try babysitting websites, too, if the options are dwindling. Many offer background checks, categorize sitters based on experience, include CPR certification, and boast other credentials that will reassure you that your child is in good hands.

The biggest excuse as to why women don't take time for themselves is because they say they don't have the budget and time for it. I challenge that. What it boils down to is you not valuing yourself enough to make yourself a priority. There are creative solutions to this. If money is tight, another option is to swap sitting services. Watch your friend's kids for the night, and the following week, let them watch yours. Or pay in services. I am positive you have something to offer a sitter as compensation.

Another thing I have learned from moving and living all over the world is to get to know your neighbors. It's convenient, and they are generally available in emergency or desperate situations. Bring them some baked goods (store bought totally counts!), invite them over, or get to know them in passing. It's a bonus if they have kids of their own or are empty nesters because they will be so much more understanding and inclined to help out.

If you hire someone to help, use your time wisely. Wisely may mean that you hire a sitter so you are able to run errands alone. Wisely could also mean that you take a nap, read a book, or sit in silence untouched and uninterrupted. Maurice and I have hired a sitter for game days. In Russia, we received a referral for a wonderful nanny. It was my first time using a sitter, and finding ourselves in a foreign country, I was a little skeptical, but his teammate from the previous year used her and swore by her.

On game days, I went through our usual routine and took my daughter to the games with me. Yeah, Juniper was up past her bedtime, but it's okay. Right after the games, we would put her down for bed ourselves and have the sitter literally sit in our living room since Juniper was sleeping through the night. I prefer this in all honestly. I don't feel like I am missing out on time with my little, and it is one hundred percent guilt-free (note that all time away should feel guilt-free). On occasion, after she turned one, we let the sitter put her to bed. I generally chose not to go that route often because I thoroughly enjoyed our time breastfeeding and reading before bed. Either way, I found what worked for me. I was able to enjoy a kid-free dinner with my husband after home games.

On the late game days, I would put Juniper to bed and the sitter came, and I went to the games alone. Ahhh, I get chills just thinking about it! I actually watched the game and saw all of the baskets Maurice scored instead of digging in my purse for snacks, toys, lotion and chapstick. My sitter would also come when my husband was out of town just to give me relief for a couple of hours. I would take myself out on a date or get my nails done because that was a whole two-hour process (totally worth it though because they looked ahh-mazing and lasted up to three weeks), meet up with a friend, leisurely try on clothes, or just do nothing.

As you build your community, keep in mind that women need women. This was extremely apparent in Senegal and something western society is missing. It was more efficient and an easier way to do things with the help of many. So build your lady tribe. Not only can we share the weight of the tasks at hand if we have a support system, but women possess special healing properties. Women are emotional and have divine energy. Women are supreme healers and lovers and mothers. You are an oracle. You are a divine creature, a feminine spirit, and a light. It only makes sense to surround yourself with other divine, healing beings in order to rise higher and collectively support one another. Together, the force is unstoppable.

CHAPTER 12:

Okay, Now What?

Hopefully, you can see the simplicity of this *8-Step Model* and how it will help you feel supported and capable in your unique familial situation. The question is do you truly want to solve this problem? Do you want to feel like you are capable of raising your family while your husband is constantly traveling? Are you ready to find your own identity separate from your roles as wife and mother? Or do you want to continue seeking sympathy from others and feeding off of the sympathy you receive while subsequently starving yourself of self-love? Do you find satisfaction in victimizing yourself? Are you really ready to make the effort to build a lady tribe? Maybe you think it will get better on its own over time or after he retires from playing, but you still will have unresolved issues brewing underneath the surface, causing inevitable disconnect. Perhaps you are content suffering alone. And that's totally okay . . . if that works for you. But let me say something: If that worked for you in the past, you probably wouldn't have even opened up this book in the first place.

This model requires you to choose a true statement instead of allowing the story you've created be the truth. You must be completely transparent, honest, open, and objective. This seems to be a common obstacle for many women. Clients always revert back to how their husbands don't try anymore to help out, when really the truer statement is they aren't sure how their wives want him to better support them.

"He barely talks to me so he's doesn't care about me." The truer statement is that he has trouble listening to long stories at the end of the day after he's mentally checked out. It is challenging to find the truer statement especially when this entire time, you have been listening to your psyche and the made up stories in your head rather than the truths that will better serve you. It's hard to find the truth in your situation when you have friends feeding into that story you created. I assure you that with practice it will become second nature.

A recap of the *8-Step Model*:

1. Acknowledge Your Situation: As your caregiver archetype dominates, you take on many roles within your family—wife, mom, secretary, accountant, assistant, housekeeper, chef, support system, taxi driver, business partner, rock, and the glue that holds it all together. But remember the role(s) you play get to look however you want them to look. You get to define your family structure and dynamics. You have the power to choose. In the most helpless situations, you feel like your hands our tied. You feel stuck. That stuck feeling will keep you from putting action to the "8 Steps." But you are not stuck because you have to power to choose.

2. Find Your Triggers: Are you actually aware of your triggers and how they affect your reactions to high-pressure situations? When understanding why you are so bothered by the lack of contribution, most people can identify the root of their triggers, but do not know how to use this information to their benefit. That's where coaching can come into play.

3. Say Goodbye to the Old You: Mourn your old self and let go of the person you were before kids. Breaking old patterns and ways of

thinking is the most difficult part of this entire process. You will experience many unraveling of layers, and it takes time and practice. It's a constant evolution.

4. Say Hello, Beautiful: Shift your mindset and reclaim yourself as you give gratitude to all that was and create space for all that is. Define your new identity.

5. Mother Yourself: You have to really mother yourself and love yourself enough to prioritize yourself. It's so much more than superficial self-care. Love all up on yourself in all the ways.

6. See His Side: Remember to look at the situation from his perspective, which helps you to be objective and to find the truer statement.

7. Manage His Cameos: You will need to find that balance and routine when he's around and not around. Try not to fight against what is but embrace it. Just be flexible and surrender.

8. Build Your Support: Getting him to help out and building your support system is essential. Reaching out for help can be intimidating but allow yourself to ask for a helping hand.

Feeling overwhelmed in raising your family is debilitating. Waking up vibrant, excited, and ready to go is invaluable. It is something that can ease your life tremendously, and it is something that you didn't realize weighs on you until it's gone. It breaks my heart to see women suffering in silence because they are ashamed to voice their needs and embarrassed to ask for help. Feeling overwhelmed and alone can cost you your joy, energy, organization, and mood. Once you have support, you will feel understood and see how much more you enjoy providing for your family with a full cup.

We need more women willing to say, "I have been there and you can always talk to me without judgment." Your support system should make you feel understood and heard. That's what my framework and coaching programs do. I share tools and techniques that give relief. I create a container for your unfolding. I hold a sacred space for you to rise to your divinity.

The most detrimental pitfall after reading this book is not taking any action. Reading a book isn't magically going to improve your situation; you have to do something about what you've learned. You have to apply the framework and do the work. You have all of the tools you need to start your journey, to feel supported and capable of raising your family. You can begin to transform your life now. You are empowered to make the changes you need to make. However, I want to help you get there a lot faster and easier. Reach out to me for free supplemental resources, learn more about how to join my exclusive collective of women, and receive updates on my latest program.

CHAPTER 13:

Building Your Future

You are not alone. My hope is that you feel empowered and supported in raising your family after reading this. I wish for you to find your purpose and manifest your purposeful life into existence. I hope you have confidence in yourself and trust in your ability to raise your family. Know that you are capable, and you are enough. I hope you become your truest self, living purposefully regardless of who you were conditioned to be. My wish for you is to heal traumas—personal and generational.

After reading this book, you will know that whatever rings true to your heart's center can be accomplished once you commit to yourself. You will feel an abundance of love, light, positivity, and opportunity in your life thereafter.

I know many women are struggling out there with this same problem. I had yet to find a support group for women in my unique situation. I have befriended many beautiful souls over the years on each team my husband has played. I genuinely connect with these women, and we share in similar experiences. It appears that we all have had to struggle with the same issues. We all feel like the weight of raising our children and the weight of the household fell all on us. Essentially, we were doing this on our own. Our husbands were hardly around, and even when they were present, they weren't really present. Their minds were elsewhere, preparing for the next day at practice or the upcoming game or recovering their bodies or just mentally checking out because the week has been so stressful. This is how my book was born—through meeting so many women in the same boat as me who thought they were alone and the only ones going through this. We've all experienced, to some degree, the same issues and didn't have any resources to pull from.

I hope you see that you, too, can get past this rocky road and find a way to enjoy and embrace your life. I hope you now understand that a traditional family dynamic isn't the only way to make a marriage work. I hope you choose to define your family dynamic. It gets to look however you want it to look. I also wanted to show women in this position that it's okay to do things for yourself.

I feel called to those who are lost and wrapped up in your role as a wife and mom, so much that you forgot who you are. I feel called to help those who cannot seem to balance life and the great responsibility of raising babies and being supportive wives. I wrote this book for you, the one swimming with overwhelm, feeling like you can't ever get anything right.

I wrote this book for you who feel like you are not enough—not enough of a mother to your children and not enough of a wife to your husband. I wrote this book to remind you that you are enough. I wrote this book to give you permission to feel all of the feels and move toward finding solutions. This book creates a container that allows you to feel, reflect, forgive, grow, heal, and elevate. I wrote this book so that you would feel heard and understood. This book creates a sense of community, a safe space for you to connect and receive the support you desperately need.

I wrote this book because I couldn't find a community that I felt comfortable sharing this part of me with. No one seemed to understand what I was going through. Yes, to a certain extent they were able to sympathize for me, but they never really experienced or had to live it. I wanted to create a book that could translate into a program. That program then creates a community of women sharing their stories, finding their voices, discovering themselves, and reclaiming their lives in a safe, sacred space.

In this sacred space, we all listen, and speak from our hearts. There is a fine line between airing your dirty laundry/putting your business all out there and sharing what you're going through. No one wants to throw their husbands under the bus or dog them publicly. But we also need some constructive outlet to let those feelings out. I wrote this book because there is a need for a safe, sacred space for us to lift one another up, encourage, cry with, celebrate, and relate. I wrote this book because the world desperately needs vulnerability.

I wrote this book so that I could heal myself. I wrote this book to liberate myself from all of the burdens and weight of my fears. I feel called to pass down wisdom and share my knowledge so that I can help countless women. It is such a blessing to be able to help even one woman with my words.

I wrote this book because my contributions matter in this world. No one can tell my story the way I can. I wrote this book because I have a purpose. I am called to facilitate healing. I am a healer who empowers others to heal themselves. I empower others to empower themselves. I am a Lightworker. I spread light.

Thank You

Thank you for taking the time to read my book. I love you for opening it, and I applaud you for finishing the whole book! You are a beautiful soul!

Motherhood can be a delicate balance, and I want to support you as much as possible. As a special way to show my gratitude toward you, I'd love to gift you a free connection call. I have laid out the simple process that works time and time again whenever things feel a little out of whack. The hard part is the work that is required in each step, which is why I am here to help. If you are overwhelmed, exhausted, and maybe even isolated, I would love to create a strategic plan and equip you with the tools needed to ride the ebbs and flows of motherhood effortlessly. At the end of the connection call, you will know it's possible to shake the overwhelm and stress, find life balance, and feel supported while raising your family.

Schedule your free connection call at HardlyHomeBook.com/schedule.

About the Author

Kelsey Domiana is an intuitive life coach and yoga instructor who helps women struggling to balance raising a family, being a supportive wife, and showing up for themselves. She makes a daily conscious effort to remain grounded and balanced while her husband is always on the go as a professional basketball player. Between living abroad and stateside for his job, Kelsey uses creativity, connection, and communication to make their lifestyle work. It's not without its challenges, and through her virtual one-on-one programs, she shares the wisdom she's collected from their adventures. She has created a tribe of mamas with similar family dynamics.

Her yoga journey started as a way to enhance her performance as a professional basketball player. It was a low-impact way to build strength, release tension in neglected muscles, tendons, and fascia, enhance mind-body connection, and breathe correctly. Game changer. Along the way she became certified in Hatha yoga, and now, her yoga practice focuses on exploring the union of breath and movement. This has catapulted her spiritual journey and energy awakening as a Lightworker.

She is a magnetic force who truly believes that heart-centered work creates magic. She teaches yoga workshops at Youth Basketball and Empowerment camps in Senegal, Africa, annually. Making yoga accessible to those who otherwise wouldn't have access to it ignites her.

The most rewarding part of her yoga journey is sharing it with her one-year-old daughter, Juniper. They explore breath-led movement together through meditation, asanas, and babywearing yoga. She fastens Juniper onto her with a wrap that encourages a sacred bond and celebrates the beauty and divinity of motherhood called Reclaim Woven. Currently, Kelsey teaches Hatha, meditation, prenatal, and babywearing yoga in Scottsdale, Arizona and coaches clients online.

Kelsey attended Miami University for her undergraduate degree and Purdue University for her graduate degree. She is the CEO of the Maurice Ndour Foundation.

She aims to inspire, empower, and support other women on their journeys, bringing warmth, safety, and a welcoming vibe to all.

Email: kelsey.domiana@gmail.com
Instagram: @kdomiana